Reflections

Reflections

MARGARET G. A. ALEXANDER

LitPrime
"Your story is our priority"

LitPrime Solutions
21250 Hawthorne Blvd
Suite 500, Torrance, CA 90503
www.litprime.com
Phone: 1-800-981-9893

Published by LitPrime Solutions   06/02/2022

ISBN: 979-8-88703-015-9(sc)
ISBN: 979-8-88703-016-6(e)

Library of Congress Control Number: 2022909493

In loving memory of:

Margaret G. A. Alexander

September 20, 1924 – June 03, 2022

Contents

Dedication

The book is dedicated to:

SON, Kelly Miller Alexander, Jr.
SON, Alfred Louis Alexander

And

A Devoted Daughter-in-Law,
Helen T. Anthony Alexander

Also To:

* * *   GRANDSONS   * * *
Nathanael Maurice Alexander
Kelly Miller Alexander, III
Desmond Phifer

GREAT GRANDCHILDREN
Cloey Barnes and Aiden Isaiah Phifer

Prologue

WELCOME AND THANK you for taking time to share my reminiscences with me. I'm thinking you'll find the book an interestingly easy read taking you on my life's journey. It's really a "thumb-nail" or "birds-eye" view of my upbringing and experiences: Educational, Spiritual, Social and Recreational. There's also a look at my community service activities and family lifestyle. It has historical facts and connection with various individuals, numerous family members and friends. You'll find bits and pieces of information, here and there, to surprise, make you smile or even laugh. There are photographs that will help you understand how folk lived "back-in-the-day". There's insight to the author's transition from childhood to adulthood.

I chose writing this book, as a way, to leave my footprints in the sands-of-time with the hope that my spirit will be lasting.

Enjoy the read!

Mrs. Margaret Gilreece Alexander Alexander

T HROUGHOUT THE YEARS, various individuals have said to me, "You should write a book." Recently, my sons, Kelly, Jr. and Alfred and grandson Kelly, III encouraged me to do so. Today, I decided to take pen in hand and put my thoughts on paper; my preference is old fashion yellow legal pads rather than the computer. Kelly, Jr. jokingly says, "I'm going to get you a box of quill pens to really make you comfortable".

The main event for Alberta Wallace and Eulie Lester Gilreece Alexander on September 20, 1924 was the birth of their daughter, Margaret Gilreece Alexander. This year I will be 90 years old.

It is increasingly hard for young people, and at my age that's just about everybody not born in the "roaring 20's" to imagine what life was like before cell phones, computers, tweets and instant messages. But to understand my story, you must wrap your arms around a world where white women had just received the right to vote a scant four years before I joined the world; a world where World War I had exposed thousands of black men to a world "over there", where they were judged more by what they could do than by the color of their skin; world in restless transition from "Jim Crow" to what would during my lifetime become the dawning of equality.

What was happening in 1924? "Nellie T. Ross of Wyoming and Mirian A. "Ma" Ferguson of Texas were the first women to be elected as state governors; Congress conferred U. S. citizenship to all native-born Indians, while ignoring the festering sore of African

American second class citizenship and denial of the right to vote throughout the South.

On September 28th, two U.S. Army airplanes touched down in Seattle, Washington, having completed the first round-the-world flight in 175 days. In a lighter note, Lionel Steinberger puts a slice of cheese on a hamburger patty in Pasadena, California, creating the first recorded cheeseburger. Eighty nine years later we would be debating the nutritional value of fast food and the sanity of eating too many of Mr. Steinberger's creations.

The Eulie Lester Gilreece Alexander family resided at 709 East Eleven Street, between North Alexander & North Myers Streets, immediately behind Mt, Moriah Primitive Baptist Church on the corner of North Alexander & East 11th Streets in Charlotte, North Carolina. Try as you might, only an archeological dig will let you find the house now. The march of progress, in this case the construction of the Brookshire freeway and the forced removal of black folk from the downtown environs buried the home of my youth somewhere under the crushed stone, rebar and concrete of the freeway. Though my immediate neighborhood is gone, its memory lingers on.

My childhood was happy and enjoyable. I received parental love, protection and guidance. I was provided with everything a young girl could imagine. Looking back, I can't remember wanting for anything reasonable or unreasonable. Don't tell anybody, but by today's standards, I was quite possibly a spoiled brat.

One of my sons accuses me to this day of having perfected the technique of getting my way. "From the little girl pout to the old lady near sighted squint, whatever works", I say. "Use what you've got with class and a smile".

Originally, we lived in a three room house with hallway and a toilet on the back porch. The long front porch with banisters was the width of the house with a wooden glider on one side of the front door and three wooden chairs (1 large & 2 medium) on the opposite side. Later, two rooms and a bathroom were added and the front porch was tiled; as well as underpinning the entire house with brick.

The house was usually painted white or a shade of yellow trimmed in brown.

In our front yard were a large acorn shade tree and a small Pomegranate tree. Years later, as urban renewal forced my parents to move, my father planted that Pomegranate tree in my yard on Senior Drive. I don't know if it was more a gift for me or the kids, but he planted it and it's still there bearing fruit. Every time I look out my window it brings back fond memories of my father. Just thinking about the old house and yard reminds me of how handy he was. I took for granted all the things he could do with his hands; things that today I have to call a professional to come out to the house to do.

In our back yard there was a chinaberry tree which I enjoyed climbing and sitting in while eating the sweet yellow substance from a locus recently taken off another tree. Today, I do not see any locus trees anymore. However, I saw one in Fayetteville, North Carolina many years ago while attending a North Carolina State Conference of NAACP Branches convention there.

I am reminded of a beautiful Magnolia Tree in our backyard now on Senior Drive. This huge tree was planted around 1963 by my sons, Kelly, Jr. and Alfred. From my kitchen window, I pointed out to the kids exactly where I wanted it; in the center of the backyard.

The tree was a gift from Charles McLean, Field Director, North Carolina, National Association for the Advancement of Colored People (NAACP), from Winston-Salem, NC. A half century later, the enormous exquisite tree with shiny green leaves and large white flowers, towers high toward the sky and can be seen from Beatties Ford Road far above the Shopping Center buildings among the trees in the background. It's a wonderful sight to see.

Homes when I was growing up used a privy instead of a toilet or bathroom. A locked privy accommodated two to six homes in the neighborhood; primitive conditions by modern standards, but the norm back in the day; so much the norm that it went unremarked and unnoticed. It is only in looking back that the communal privy seems somehow out of place. Indoor toilets were still the preserve of the well-to-do.

The Saturday night bath is a frontier cliché' but my parents and our neighbor's heated water and poured it in a large tin tub in order to take a bath once a week, usually on a Saturday evening before going to bed. It was Saturday night because you wanted to be clean as a whistle for Sunday Church services. A small wash pan or bowl was used during other days. Chamber pots or slop-jars with a lid were used over-night if needed because it was a long lonely walk in the dark of night to the communal privy. Some of you young folk, reading this will think that we must have used candles to provide illumination at night. Not so, kerosene lamps were common providing a soft diffused light.

Our home was located on a steep dirt road which ran down a hill about two blocks, where it intersected, with another dirt road along the banks of Little Sugar Creek. Flooding was a regular occurrence. Even today there is a small amount of flooding in the area after a hard rain storm.

One of my husband's brothers, Louis was fond of saying, "You don't get educated to be ignorant". Looking at the television the other day, seeing pictures of flooded streets and remembering how many fine homes are flooded each year because we build in flood plains remind me of Louis and his saying. Segregation forced many of us to live in undesirable locations, but over the years greed has made us forget common sense.

Sugar Creek is paved over now. Charlotte, they say, buries a lot of its history, paving it over with asphalt and concrete. Sometimes, they just tear it down and build something new and shiny. This will stand the test of time, until something newer and shinier comes along.

Today the revitalization of Little Sugar Creek is part of the next new thing. Brown Row lives in my imagination...the wooden bridge over the creek leading to the brown wood frame row houses precariously perched on brick pillows, which resembled the stilt houses of the Everglades. When it rained, the creek would rise up, drowning the bridge, flowing like the Catawba under the houses,

Bordering the creek, where a grassy playing field is today, was what to my child's eye, was acres of brown clay. I fondly remember how every year a carnival set up in this field. Everyone in the neighborhood it seemed would come out to enjoy the rides. My favorite was the carousel, round-n-round it went, calipee music filling the air, inviting one and all to hop on board and let your imagination soar.

That magic field presented itself to some of my friends as a place to dine. The field itself was sampled by some, who just loved the taste and feel of red clay rolling around in their mouths. Some of the old folks talked about everyone sampling "a peck of dirt" before being taken up in that heavenly chariot to be with the Lord. Today, we know that some people crave red clay because of a mineral deficiency.

My grand ma, whom I called Momma Lula, Aunt Odessa and Uncle "Sonny" Walter, lived across the street from the carnival grounds at 928 E. 10th St. Momma Lula kept a supply of white mini balls of mint candy for me to eat on my frequent visits. She taught me how to wash dishes. A strait chair turned backwards at the kitchen table for me to stand on. Three large pans of water were on the table for me to wash and then rinse the dishes twice.

I was in the fifth grade at Alexander Street Elementary School, corner of East 12th St. & North Alexander St., when Momma Lula died. Soon after her death, Aunt Odessa moved across the street from us on Eleventh St. and Uncle Walter relocated to New York City to be near his brother, Uncle James Clarence Wallace.

Family surrounded me in first ward "Cody Town": Great Aunt Eugenia and Uncle Mack Jackson and six cousins[1] on East 10th St.; Aunt Cora "Sis" and Uncle Tom Massey and five cousins[2] also on East 10th St.; Aunt Odessa "Love" & Uncle Buddy Young lived on North Alexander Street and operated a small variety store located beside their home.

In Cody Town almost everybody knew each other and was familiar with every street, alley, lane and shortcut throughout the community.

Children were taught to respect, obey and respond to their elders with "yes Mam' or no Sir", often doors were left unlocked, screened windows left open and people slept on their porch on a hot summer night without fear. Kids were competitive and creative. On special occasions, we memorized Bible verses, made-up plays and stories, participated in talent shows and pretended to be schoolteachers, store managers or chief cooks. We were great at using our imaginations.

We enjoyed a verity of games: (i.e. Softball, Hide & Seek, Jack Stones, Hop Scotch, Little Sally Walker, Mary Mack Dressed in Black; worked picture puzzles and played with paper dolls). We attended invitation only birthday celebrations. Our party games were: Pen-the-tail-on-the-donkey while blindfold; dunking for apples in a tubful of water; spin-the-bottle; dancing and eating ice-cream, cake, peanuts, mints and drinking punch or lemonade. My friends were always welcome at our home. We had the space and I had lots of toys and games to play with.

My favorite Bible verse was "Honor thy father and thy mother, that your days be long upon the land which the Lord thy God giveth thee". This is a shorter version of **Deuteronomy 5:16**.

During this period, the city limit of Charlotte stopped at Beatties Ford Road and I believe, LaSalle St.

As I grew older, there were long streetcar rides to the end of the line in Northwest Charlotte and back home to First Ward or "Cody Town". The streetcar fare was .07 cents; a transfer at the square (Intersection of Tryon & Trade Streets) was .05 cent. A great outing on a Sunday afternoon was a long walk to the Armory Auditorium, which was later named the Grady Cole Center and then Park Center. Where we sat on the grass, took pictures, strolled about and just talked. On the return home, we stopped by the pharmacy, on East Seventh Street, for an ice cream cone, cup or sandwich to slowly savor.

On Saturday, we walked to the Lincoln Theater on East Second Street for a matinee movie; after which we'd walk back home discussing what we had just seen at the movies.

Sunday was an all-day affair, church activities consisted of: Sunday School 9:45 am; Morning Service – 11:00 am; a church club or group sponsored program – 3:00 pm; Baptist Young Peoples

Union (BYPU) – 5:00 pm and Evening Worship Service – 6:00 pm with an obligatory Prayer meeting on Wednesday evenings.

Back –in-the-day children got lots of exercise walking and really enjoyed doing it. Seemingly, today's youth prefer riding and sitting rather than walking. Perhaps that's a factor in the growth of obesity.

++++++++++++++++++++

In the First Ward area bounded by East Seventh Street to immediately past East Twelfth Street to the railroad tracks there were approximately four major churches and four prayer houses; Mount Moriah Primitive Baptist Church (corner of North Alexander and East Eleven Streets), Gilfield Baptist Church (on North Myers Street between East Ninth & East Tenth Streets), Little Rock A.M.E. Zion Church (corner of North Myers & East Seventh Streets) and Seven Street Presbyterian Church[3] located at the corner of East Seventh & North College Streets.

Prayer Houses[4] were located (on North Alexander St. between E. 10th & E. 11th Streets); (on E. 12th between N. Alexander & N. Myers Streets); (on E. 10th St. between N. Siegel Ave. & Little Sugar Creek) and (on the corner of E. 10th St. & N. Alexander Street). I do not recall the name of the Prayer Houses.

Often between church services at Mt. Moriah Primitive Baptist Church some members stood in the shade of our giant acorn tree or sat on our front porch. My mother was an excellent cook and always had food to share. Momma's biscuits, pies and cakes were delicious. On Sunday there were always two meats; chicken and either beef, veal or pork roasts. Daddy raised chickens and pigeons[5]; there was a smokehouse in our back yard. Frequently, I rode with daddy in his truck to feed our hogs in the country. When the hogs were slaughtered, momma made liver mush, souse meat, sausage and crackling. My favorite dinner was greens, sweet potatoes, cornbread with fried or baked chicken, pork or veal chops, brisket stew meat or spare ribs.

Messrs. Ike and Jim, elder gentlemen, lived down the hill from us on 11th St. Each owned a horse and wagon. Church groups sponsored hayrides which were very popular in our neighborhood there were approximately ten grocery stores, mainly operated by whites, one ice & coal house on N. Davidson St. and one large boarding house on E. 10th St. Vendors sold fresh vegetables, bottle flavorings; bed linen, cosmetics, ice, coal and wood. [6] Ordered milk and butter were delivered to your door once a week. Now, it is convenient for us to purchase milk or butter at a store when needed.

Today, First Ward has been rebuilt, revamped and revitalized. Gone forever is "Cody Town", but it still lives in my memory. It is a mystery to me as to why First Ward from East 9th to 12th Street was commonly called "Cody Town". As a girl growing up, I just accepted the name and never bothered to ask its' origin.

Before October 1, 2012, nobody I asked was able to answer my question of: "Why was a portion of First Ward referred to as "Cody Town"? However, Mrs. Rosalie Davis Meeks age 87, now lives in University Park, provided the answer. She said, "Mr. Cody, a wealth white man, bought-up a large portion of land and built a huge number of shot-gun houses on the property."

Rosalie is the sister of Robert "Bob" Davis who was 83 in 2012. The three of us grew-up in First Ward and attended Mount Moriah Primitive Baptist Church. Robert served as an educator with the Charlotte Mecklenburg Schools from 1936 – 1991, when he retired as Principal. He served as Chairman, Black Leadership Caucus founded in 1976; Former Chairman, Charlotte Mecklenburg County Black Political Caucus; Past Chairman, Charlotte-Mecklenburg County National Association for the Advancement of Colored People (NAACP) Education Committee and Vice-Chair, Wilmore Community Organization.

Rosalie D. Meeks says: "I've come a long way from where I started. I'm so grateful, thankful and blessed." Although her husband died recently and is greatly missed, she's extremely proud of the accomplishments and achievements of their off-springs and grandchildren.

Rosalie talks rapidly and remembers much about the people who lived in First Ward many years ago. We talked about every nook and cranny in the area. It would have been great to have taped our telephone conversation. Since I did not, I'm writing bits and pieces regarding our discussion. I was somewhat perturb when Rosalie D. Meeks revealed that growing-up she considered herself poor while I was " the little rich girl" whose parents gave her everything. I had no idea that she felt that way until now. Believe it or not, I am not rich and never have been rich but have always lived well and successfully managed what was provided for me by my parents, my husband and our Heavenly Father, God. For that I am eternally thankful and grateful. It is my belief that the universe is activated to shower us with more when we are conscious of and grateful for what we have.[Z]

+++++++++++++++++++

I spoke with my friend, Mrs. Ann Gallmon Hunter, to get her impression on living in First Ward as a very young girl. Her response was, "Oh! I loved First Ward. We were like "one big happy family" there. My Mother always taught me and my brother to be neighborly. Today, I'm living in "Hyde Park", in northwest Charlotte, NC, where all of us in the area are like family too."

Ann and I are members of Alpha Lambda Omega Chapter, Alpha Kappa Alpha Sorority, Inc. She is a retired school teacher. Ann and her late husband, Wright Hunter, Jr., are members of Little Rock A.M.E. Zion Church, Charlotte, NC. They have one daughter, Brianna.

Wright Hunter, Jr. was, also, a good friend of mine. I admire his integrity, pride, honor and helpfulness. We "claimed kin" to each other. As I am, he was a native of Charlotte, NC. He died August 23, 2007. Wright was known as a master teacher, a tough grader who demanded the best from his students. He was a crusader for justice and what he believed to be right. His favorite quotation from lawyer, Clarence Darrow who fought for human justice was: "And what does the Lord require of you? To act justly and to love mercy and to walk humbly with your God". Micah 6:8

++++++++++++++++++++

I also spoke with Theoplis Ingram in order to get his viewpoint regarding growing up in First Ward. He reminisced,

"My childhood in First Ward will always be a part of my memories. It is a part of me that will always be there. It was a neighborhood of closely knit families. Everybody knew each other. It was a neighborhood with sections within the neighborhood. Such as, Mosquito Bottoms, normally called "The Bottoms", and Ryan's Row just to name a few. From an infant, Mt. Moriah Primitive Baptist Church was my family church. Ms. Isabell Stevenson was my first Sunday school teacher. She taught us as children to always be kind to others. When I became of age, my father, Cub Master, started me scouting. Mrs. Bessie Hudson worked along with my father.

I became a Boy Scout under Mr. Jimmy Diggs. He was a good leader for all the boys in Troop #73. Bobby Stevenson and I attained the rank of Eagle Scout. Sterling Woodard was a member of our Troop but not our church also was an Eagle Scout. I thank my parents for teaching me the values of being obedient and respectful to others. Alexander Street Elementary School was located in First Ward. Mrs. Jannie Wallace Hemphill was Principal. She and all the teachers had all students in their hearts and made every effort to teach us.

I can't forget "Didley's Cafe" on North Alexander Street. It was a popular gathering spot for adults. One could get Bubble Gum for one cent and a Nehi Grape or Orange Drink for ten cent. I recall many families had credit at grocery stores: i.e., The Creek Store, Limburger's, Hubbard's and Covington's. All in all, First Ward was great. I'm sure I've missed some things but First Ward will always be in my heart and mind."

Theoplis is now in his mid-seventies, retired after employment for thirty years at Alexander Funeral Home, Inc. serving as Funeral Director, General Manager of Operations and Assistant Vice

President. He married his high school sweetheart, Mary Lou Roach and they produced two sons and two daughters. He is a grandfather to ten and great-grandfather to eleven children.

I telephoned my cousin, Helen Jackson Laurel in Central Islip, New York, today and we talked almost an hour about her childhood in Charlotte, North Carolina. Helen is now age 80 and has a family of four adult females and three adult males. At this point, Helen uses a walker and is in the process of having some extensive dental work done. She's wondering about the expense and trying to think of a way to solve her problem. Seemingly, only two of her adult children occasionally contribute a little financial support.

When I inquired concerning her impression of growing up in First Ward in Charlotte, NC, she immediately said, "I wanted to get away from there".

It seems that sometimes her father, Uncle Mack Jackson, was unfaithful to her mother, Aunt Eugenia Jackson, with other women; thus, creating a problem. Aunt Eugenia and family relocated to New York City when Helen was age 12. Helen attended West Charlotte High School for six months, when the school was located on Beatties Ford Road.

Helen revealed to me that her father drank whiskey and would give some to his kids occasionally. Helen said, "I liked the taste". She went on to say that, one day her nephew, Howard Jackson went to Alexander Street Elementary School drunk and the Principal, Ms. Janie Hemphill, confronted Howard. He told Ms. Hemphill that his grandfather gave him the whiskey and gave Helen some too. The Principal had a conference with all concerned and promised to report the matter to the Administrative Authority if this ever occurred again.

Aunt Eugenia Jackson was indeed a quiet, gentle, modest and kind christen woman. As the expression goes, "She would not hurt a flee". In my opinion, Uncle Mack took advantage of her kindness and her love for him. Oh! Yes, Uncle Mack was known to be a Preacher and preached sometime at a small prayer house on East Tenth Street. Can you imagine that? I suppose that's what they called "A Jack Leg Preacher".

Also, Cousin Helen recalled that she gave each of her sons and daughters, while they were youngsters, a bottle or glass of whiskey or beer and had each one drink every drop of it all at once. At another time, Helen gave each one a whole pack of cigarettes and saw to it that they smoked every cigarette in the package – one cigarette behind another until the pack was empty. She thought this would prevent them from wanting to drink whiskey or smoke cigarettes in the future. One of her daughters said, "Ma, you made me the woman I am today". Helen remembers that it helped some of her children but it didn't do any good for others. We win some and we lose some! - As the saying goes. For the record, I'm not in favor of that example; but to each – his or her own.

Mildred Jeanette McCullough Alexander, my favorite sister-in-law, a sincere friend and Soror, whom I felt very close to and was very much like "the sister I never had ". I've never met a person who says anything derogatory about Mildred. Even the students she taught at Morgan Elementary School in the Cherry section in Charlotte, NC have a good report and speak well of Mildred's character, personality and teaching. I tell you, she was one of a kind." She made me feel like "a member of the family" from the beginning. She knew how to put one at ease. She was welcoming and hospitable.

Mildred was a teacher for thirty-three years in the Charlotte Public schools and retired in 1967. She and Zack, Jr. married June 14, 1927. They produced two sons: Zack Wilbur and Andrew.

She was deeply religious and gave freely of her time to promote the work of her church, Saint Paul Baptist. She was a charter member of the Alpha Lambda Omega Chapter of Alpha Kappa Alpha Sorority; a member of the Cosmopolitan Club, the Friendly Girls Club and Charlotte Camp No. 1, the American Woodmen.

She attended school and spent her early childhood in Wheeling, West Virginia. Her college work was done at the New England Conservatory of Music, Boston, Massachusetts, Howard University, Washington, D. C. and Columbia University, New York, New York.

Mildred was thoughtful and helpful. When Kelly, Jr. was about age four, she took him to visit her family in Wheeling, West Virginia for a week or so. She taught Kelly, Jr. how to plant a vegetable garden. Also, she helped with his school work during the summer vacation period. She was there helping to clean up the kitchen after the family Christmas dinner. I didn't drive therefore, we road together for our Sorority meetings. We could count on each other. My dear friend has gone to be with God, our Heavenly Father, but she is not forgotten.

De Rosette Yvonne Hendricks Blunt, born July 6, 1934, was my husband's favorite cousin, I believe. Her parents are Velma and Ernest Hendricks. After Velma's parents died, she came to live with my husband's parents, who were her Uncle and Aunt. Therefore, Velma grew up with my husband and his brothers. Poppa's brother was Velma's father

Both, Kelly, Sr. and I are fond of De Rosette, who we affectionately call "Derrie". In 1956, Derrie married a newly minted First Lieutenant Roger R. Blunt, who rose to the rank of Major General; after which, she visited with Kelly, Sr. and I at 415 E. Stonewall Street in Charlotte, NC. For a few weeks while Roger was doing some type of training farther south. All of us kept in touch by letters and visits before Derrie died in 2007.

DeRosette and her younger brother, Adrain, grew up in Rutherford, New Jersey on Eastern Way. She was an all around student; excelling academically while participating in sports and music activities. She graduated from Weaton College in Norton, Massachusetts on a full scholarship; graduated Magna Cum Laude with a B.A. in Political Science, a major in History and was elected to the Phi Beta Kappa Society. She received the International Relations Scholarship during her days at Weaton, and used it to study Contemporary English Literature & Polities at the University of Oxford in England.

Derrie was a community activist. She served as Precinct Captain and member of the Alexandria Democratic City Committee. She was secretary of the Virginia 8th District Democratic Committee and President of the 8th District Black Caucus.

During the 1980's Derrie became President, Metropolitan Washington Ministry with Women. She was top producer on the President's Membership Council of the Greater Washington Board of Trade. She was a member on the Montgomery County Maryland Board of Education's Commission on Excellence in Teaching.

Derrie was active in arts. She was Treasurer, Washington Performing Arts Society's (WPAS) Women's Committee, and served as Resource Chair and Co-Corporate Liaison of the Smithsonian Women's Committee.

Derrie believed that "charity is one of humankind's ultimate accountabilities." She was involved in numerous charitable activities and outreach programs. She sponsored a child in the African village of Lipangalala, Tanzania, which included providing financial support for basic necessities. She acted as an advocate against the death penalty and established relationships with death-row inmates, providing spiritual support.

Derrie loved music. She enjoyed playing the piano. In high school, she played the snare drums and the glockenspiel in the marching band. Derrie also enjoyed singing in various choirs throughout her life. As of December 30, 2007, DeRosette Blunt is now singing in heaven with the angels. We love you, Derrie.

Various Events

I CONTACTED MY COUSIN, John Thomas "Sonny" Massey and asked him to tell me something about his experience growing up in First Ward. He and his devoted wife, Gladys Alexander Massey live in Northwest Charlotte and are active members of Friendship Missionary Baptist Church. The following is what he said:

"I started Alexander Street Elementary School at age 5 because my 6th birthday was in December. Ms. Janie Wallace Hemphill, principal was a loving person who treated students as if they were her own children. She was also very strict and called all male students "Sonny Boy" and female students "Sister". She made sure that students did not loiter in hallways; neither did she allow any running or horse-play. When she caught a student running in the halls, she loudly called out "Sonny Boy" or "Sister". You may be sure; the acting guilty individual "froze" in his or her tracks.

As punishment, Ms. Hemphill would let a student stand in a dark closet in her office to "settle down". If she could not get you to become quiet or orderly, by standing in the closet, she'd use her wooden paddle with holes in it to scare or actually sometimes hit the very unruly student. My momma taught me to be obedient or she would "handle me when I got home in the afternoon."

I loved going to school and did not miss any days unless I had measles, mumps or some other contagious disease. Our school nurse, Miss Walls constantly checked on us making sure that we did not come to school with communicable diseases.

During elementary school, I had teachers such as Miss Bamfield. She placed "fear" in you, if you did not bring in assigned homework. By going to school, and not participating in playing hooky, helped me to be regular in attendance. Upon entering into the world of work, for forty years of employment, I did not miss a day except for Hospital stays and recuperation. I retired from F.M.C.(Food, Machinery, Chemical).

When I was around twelve years old, I developed a liking for Baseball. My uncle, Eulie Lester Alexander saw my potential and helped me to develop my potentiality. I started playing baseball with a group of older men (such as: Buddy Young, Zeke Henderson, Ken Henderson, and Edward Watts among others). These men helped keep me out of trouble.

I recall Tony Cousar, who lived in Waxhaw, NC; who caught rabbits, skinned them and brought them to Charlotte, NC to be sold to people in the neighborhood. Tony knew of a Baseball Team in Waxhaw and he connected with Buddy Young, our team Manager, and we began a rivalry. We played baseball against the Waxhaw Team, as well as, Baseball Teams from surrounding areas.

Later, uncle Eulie gave me a goat because my brother, Willie and I, helped him to pick up kitchen refuse from various restaurants. The "Slop" was used to feed the Hogs that were being raised by Charlotte residents who lived in the northern part of Charlotte. I cared for that goat with care and compassion and allowed neighborhood kids to play with him.

Mount Moriah Primitive Baptist Church was the church of my family's choice. Mr. Robert Raye, Sunday School Superintendent and Mrs. Bertha Pickenpack, his mother and a Mother of the church; make me recall fond memories of church activities. Mr. Ross, Scout Master provided leadership for numerous scouting activities. We went to several places camping and hiking.

After I outgrew playing with the older men, I formed a Soft Ball Team with boys of my age. A lot of talent was discovered and we played against other teams in the city. We were great athletes and gravitated to playing Baseball. We played some nights and weekends. Initially, lights were not on in the neighborhood parks; so our games were played during the day hours. Eventually, lights were put in "Cody Town", "Beatties Ford" and "Pearl Street" parks. "Cody Town", "Mosquito Bottom" and First Ward are the same area; and were known to be the scene of many fist fights, shootings and other negatives but the Ballgames were attended by many residents of Charlotte. When we played Baseball on our home field, which was at the back of Piedmont Courts, we had a hard time keeping up with our balls. The white residents looked through the fence separating the ballpark and Piedmont Court. When players hit the ball over the fence, the young white kids would grab the balls and run without giving the ball back to us. The parents would just continue to look at the game and not make the children return the balls.

The Charlotte Clippers was the name of the Semi Pro Baseball Team that was found by me. Our first Manager was Andrew Brewton who came to us from Brooklyn. The Charlotte Clippers was a very strong team utilizing the talents of many young men from First Ward. I later became Player/Manager."

Spiritual Roots

I GREW UP GOING to Mount Moriah Primitive Baptist Church mainly with my grandmother, Mrs. Lula Conner Wallace. I called her Momma Lula. She lived down the hill and cross the street at 928 East Tenth Street. I joined Mt. Moriah in 1936 at the age of twelve having been actively involved in the church programs and activities. My spiritual roots were formed there with my parent church family. The church was the center of activities.

In the 1930's, the house between our house and Mt. Moriah Primitive Baptist Church was demolished and additions were made to the church. The balcony was taken out. Teenagers had enjoyed sitting in the balcony looking over and down at the congregation.

While the Preacher delivered a sermon, most of the congregation became exuberant; groaning, whopping and stomping their feet. The preacher always had a large white handkerchief to pull out of his pocket to wipe his face. He would receive lots of Amen's, shouting and fainting from the congregation. A favorite expression of Rev. Joseph H. Kendrick was: "My Dears".

Testifying Service was on the third Sunday morning of each month. A member started with a hymn; the congregation joined in and after which that person testified. There was no preaching that Sunday morning. However, there were numerous long meter hymns and acappella singing of spirituals. Members of Mt. Moriah were not afraid to open their mouths to sing and give vent to the Holy Sprit while praising God.

My mother, Mrs. Alberta Wallace Alexander, joined Mt. Moriah P.B. Church under the pastorate of Rev. J. J. Steele. I heard her speak of Rev. W.M. Scott, also.

Rev. Thomas F. Fraylon was pastor of Mt. Moriah during my childhood. My father, Mr. Eulie Lester Gilreece Alexander and I joined Mt. Moriah under the pastorate of Rev. Joseph H. Kendrick. In the 1940's, my father became a Deacon. He also taught Sunday school and was a Supervisor of the Boy Scouts.

Growing up, Nannie Little-Snowden, Inez Miller-Dixon, Willie Mae Waddell-Stroud and I were friendly competitors in church programs and activities. We recited speeches and sang in the choir for Easter, Mother's, Father's & Children Days and Christmas programs. Often time rehearsing at the home of Mrs. Fannie Stafford or Mrs. Jannie Baxter, the church musicians. Other pianists were: Mrs. Lottie Fraylon, Mrs. Roberta Ingram-Johnson, and Mrs. Myrtle Brewer-Johnson.

Upon graduation from Second Ward High School in 1942, I received a $25.00 Scholarship Award from the Sunday School Department; this was a large sum of money in those days.

In my adult days at Mt. Moriah, I taught Sunday school, Bible School, worked in the Missionary Circle, served on the Revival Committee, the Pastor's Appreciation Day Committee and was an active member of the Blue Rose Club while Mrs. Christine Harris was President.

Mrs. Bertha Pickenpack was my first Sunday School Teacher. She was an admirable lady who demanded respect. She kept a switch handy to lightly tap us with if we were caught talking during services. We knew to keep quiet. When the Holy Spirit moved her, she would do a whirl around and then sit down. Her son, Deacon J. Robert Raye was a Sunday School Teacher and the Superintendent. Her daughter, Mrs. Rosa Ingam and family (Husband, Burke and children, Marion, Liston, Roberta and Theoplis) were all very active church members.

During a lengthy sermon sometime you'd see Deacons W.Q. Hemphill, Henry "Bud" Ivey, Sam Mickens and Faulkner seated up front around the alter occasionally dozing. Other earlier Deacons were: Marion Cureton, Jimmy Diggs and Luther Glenn.

I remember Mrs. Mae Belle Hyatt-Newell as a well-rounded individual. She recited poems, sang solos, as well as, being in the choir and chorus and was the official writer and reader of obituaries. Mrs. Nora McLilly was a delightful lady who frequently sang soprano solos for programs and in the choir. When the Holy Spirit visited her, she would shout and fall-out usually in the choir.

Some of the senior sisters in the Amen Corner with my grandmother Lula were: Mrs. Sarah Mackey, Mrs. Martha Kelly, Mrs. Lottie Johnson, Mrs. Minnie Hudson, Mrs. Minnie Faulkner, Mrs. Minnie Ivey, Mrs. Evangeline Hemphill and Mrs. Sarah Archie. Mrs. Lottie Little sat in the middle section near the front and when she felt the Holy Spirit, she would wave her hand and pound on the back of the bench in front of her two or three times.

Mrs. Classie Rodgers and Mr. Bill Phillips ran up and down the isles when the Holy Spirit was upon them.

There was always good music at Mount Moriah; the choir was excellent, the True Vine Gospel Chorus was great and the quartet singing was outstanding. Additional choir members recalled are: Mrs. Rosa Bell Davis, Mrs. Janie & Mr. Henry Hudson, Mrs., Helen & Mr. James Dodd, Mrs. Rosa & Mr. Burke Ingram, Mrs. Elsie Brewer, Mrs. Lillie Vance, Mrs. Sally Bates, Mr. Oss Archie, Ms. Margaret and Mrs. Katherine Kendrick, Mrs. Alfreda Martin-Stafford, Mrs. Minnie Hudson and Mrs. Roberta Ingram-Johnson.

Church Clubs sold fish sandwiches, ice-cream and lemonade on the corner across the street from the church to raise funds for social projects.

The other evening I was reading over a book about the history of Mt. Moriah. When I came to the urban renewal period, you know the time when most of the inner city black neighborhoods were deemed by the powers that be to be blighted eye sores standing in the way of progress; I was struck by the value placed on the church by the city. An institution that loomed so large in the lives of the neighborhood was valued at about $50,000. That's about the value of a 800 square foot home in a modest neighborhood today. Even considering inflation, my old home church seems to have been vastly undervalued.

Elder Thomas W. Samuels assumed pastoral duties at Mt. Moriah P.B. Church in 1973. Although I am now an active member of Friendship Missionary Baptist Church, I still feel closely tired to family and friends at Mount Moriah; after all my foundation and roots were there.

Elder Samuels knew his congregation well, his sermons and casual conversation is full of references to congregants, living and dead. Not just the individuals, but who they were related to, the street they lived on and often some note worthy occurrence in their lives. You could tell by his eulogistic remarks. I continue to admire Elder T. W. Samuels and Mrs. Juanita Samuels, his devoted wife.

John Dryden says "The joys I have possessed are mine; out of thy reach, behind eternity, hid in the sacred treasure of the past, but blest remembrance brings them hourly back."[8]

Elementary School

M Y PARENTS WERE determined that I would get a better education than they had. They insisted that I study hard. To facilitate this they secured the services of a tutor, Mr. James. I don't recall his last name or where he attended school. I do remember that he was visiting Mrs. Lucy Lockhart, a neighbor of my grandma Lula, when he decided to relocate here permanently. He was a tall, thin, brown-skin, clean cut, intelligent, and literate man in his early thirties. I was required to study, master and complete my assigned school homework before I could play with my friends.

I attended Alexander Street Elementary School from first through sixth grades. My teachers were: Ms. Tyron, Mrs. Young, Ms. Price, Ms. Stevenson, Ms. Genyard and Ms. Scott.

Before I started going to school, I remember looking in the mirror with Momma while dressing and saying: "That little girl and her Momma look just like us." Of course, Momma explained to me that it was indeed our reflection in the mirror. This was either an innocent childlike imagination or a stupid ignorant assumption. I think of it as the imagination or creative ability of a young child.

Mostly, Momma plated my hair with three large plats and tired a ribbon bow on the large top plat which matched the color of the dress I was wearing that day. Sometime, Momma plated my hair in what we called "small pig tails "while at other times, she under-braided my hair. On special occasions, my hair was done in "Shirley

Temple Curls". In High School, I frequently wore a flower in my hair to match my dress. Other styles were: "Bangs" or "Page Boy".

Every morning at elementary school there was an exercise program on the radio in which the entire student body participated. The teacher stood in the doorway while the students stood in the isles next to their desks exercising. Michelle Obama would have been proud of us.

I remember the Blue Back Speller in the first grade. Each week there was approximately ten words to learn to pronounce, spell and use in a sentence or know the meaning of.

I recall being in a spelling contest in the sixth grade. Three selected students and the Principal went downtown to compete with other students from various schools throughout Charlotte-Mecklenburg County. I do not remember the exact location or who sponsored the event. However, I do remember that the four of us ate in a small room before going into the main auditorium where everyone else were seated at tables and the white students were standing in an elevated semi-circle around the room. The three of us joined in the semi-circle with the other students as the contest begun. I might add that we did not win the contest; therefore, we had to leave the room. This is about as integrated as education got in those days.

Although we were playing by the rules and regulations of that era, deep within my heart and soul I felt something was wrong with this picture. It was demeaning and disrespectful. The invitation should not have been accepted under these conditions. Indeed, it was "separate and unequal treatment." This experience placed us in a position of accepting racial segregation without realizing the situation beforehand. We should have refused to participate or protested the position. In my opinion, racial segregation is a dark part of American history.

With the clarity of hind sight, I know that my teachers must have chafed within at the indignity of it all, but yoked to the necessity of needing a job; they were bound by the injustices of the time. Revolutions start when the oppressed realize that the oppressor has no moral authority over them. That day may have been my first step along the road to rebellion against the social order.

Rumplestillskin was a story in our second grade reader. Our class put together a drama of the story and presented it at Parent-Teacher meeting one evening. I was one of the characters in the dramatization but do not recall exactly which one.

After graduation from Alexander Street Elementary School, I attended Second Ward High School from seventh through twelfth grades. There weren't any middle schools during this period.

Attending Second Ward High School

SECOND WARD HIGH School was located on the corner of South Alexander & East First Streets in a neighborhood called Brooklyn or Second Ward. Built in 1923, it was the African American community at the center of Charlotte. The school was demolished in 1960. A historic marker and memories are all that is left of the first high school for Black students in Charlotte. Nevertheless, the Second Ward High School National Alumni Foundation, Inc. is dedicated to keeping the Second Ward High School spirit alive. Its museum is located on Beatties Ford Road near its intersection with LaSalle St.in Charlotte, NC.

When the school was demolished, the board of education promised that one day a new Second Ward High would raise phoenix like from the ashes of the old. That was over fifty years ago; we're still waiting for that unfulfilled promise.

I remember vividly entering the seventh grade at Second Ward High School. Miss Mattie Hall was my homeroom teacher. From my home in First Ward, the roundtrip walk to and from school was approximately two miles. There were numerous shortcuts along the route. We usually stopped for a drink of water from the Court House fountain on E. Trade Street; then proceeded a few blocks up the hill to school.

I recall thinking, "I'm a big girl now. I've got to learn to begin standing on my own two feet, rely on my own judgment, take responsibility for my own actions and stop being a baby running home to my parents when things didn't go the way I thought they should go in school."

I had to learn to deal with problems and to think of ways to resolve them on my own. I knew I had accomplished this goal when what was a new unexpected unpleasant experience happen to me. Miss Hall slapped me on the cheek for looking out the window when she had asked the class not to do so. I did not tell my parents about the incident. I had indeed grown up. I had disobeyed an order and accepted the punishment. Previously, Miss Hall would have been called on-the-carpet or found getting-up from off-the-carpet. My mother could be a shade on the direct side at times. However, on May 25, 1942, Miss Hall wrote in my autograph book "Dear Margaret, It has been great knowing you. You are a sweet girl. Keep it up. Good Luck!"

Other homeroom teachers were: Mrs. Willie Mae Carson, who taught Home Economic; Mrs. Laura Spears Malone, also my History teacher; Mrs. Louise Spears Meadows, English; Thomas Frazier, Jr., Music; Miss Selena B. Robinson, who taught me English & Dramatics. I would describe Miss Robinson as a gentlewoman with a graceful walk.

Along the way some other instructors were: Miss Minnie Banner, English. She had this habit of tugging her jacket or girdle after diagramming a sentence on the blackboard; Mrs. Stinson taught English and insisted on students being punctual for class; Louis E. Levi, Chemistry & Physics; Edward Brown, Biology; Kenneth E. Diamond, French & Music; Mrs. M. Pettis Spivey, Mathematics and had the reputation of being really tuff in Geometry – so I regret to say, I refused to take it.; Mrs. Myrtle Brodie, History & Social Studies and was petite and very attractive; Fred L. Wiley, Journalism; Mr. O. W. Clarke, Algebra and his favorite saying was: "That's your red wagon, you can pull it or push it."; Clinton Blake, Mathematics & Dramatics; Miss Rawlings, Social Studies & Science. I remember her beautiful hands writing or drawing on the blackboard and her soft spoken voice; W. Howard Moreland, American Democracy; Miss Mans, Mrs. Mary Tyler Clarke and Mrs. Katherine Gibson Brodie McLean, Sewing. I recall her quick, fast steps while walking. After she became Mrs. McLean, our husband's worked together in the National Association for the Advancement of Colored People and we became good friends; Mrs. Carrie Robinson Quander and Mrs. Margaret Beckwith, Music.

One of my favorite teachers during this period was Mrs. Willie Mae Carson. She was a Counselor and friend whom I respected and admired. Whenever there was a problem in school, I went to her and talked it over before making the final decision. She always kept my lunch, which I brought from home, in her desk drawer until lunchtime. I usually purchased milk and a sweet bun to go with my boiled or spice ham sandwiches. Mrs. Carson also advised me on choice of college. We selected North Carolina College for Negroes (now North Carolina Central University) in Durham, NC. Another favorite teacher was Mrs. Laura Spears Malone, who was very helpful in assisting me in selecting materials, pattern and a seamstress, Mrs. Shaw to make my "1942 May Queen" dress. Mrs. Malone communicated well with students.

I took the exquisite white 1942 May Queen evening dress with me to college. After wearing it a few times, I trimmed the neckline and sleeves with black grosgrain ribbon tape for a slightly difference appearance. You may be sure; I got lots of wear out of that dress. Upon my graduation from College and marriage in 1946, I gave the dress away. At this point in life, I'm thinking that perhaps I should have held on to the dress for prosperity or for sentimental reasons. Nevertheless, I hope someone enjoyed wearing the dress as much as I did.

Some of the things I fondly remember about high school are: Singing in the school choir and being a member of the sextet; having the lead part in a 3-Act Play (a Murder Mystery Drama); being one of the dancers in the chorus line in a Broadway Musical Production, "42nd Street"; selected "May Queen" twice in a row, 1941 and 1942;

winning a prize for modeling in a fashion show, (a dress & a two-piece play set, which I made in sewing class); dissecting a frog in Biology class; member of the Debate Team; Cheerleader; enjoying football games between Second Ward & West Charlotte High schools and seeing our teachers frequently participating in plays to raise funds for the school.

Ours was the class all set for graduation from the eleventh grade in 1941 when the twelfth grade was added and the students had another year to go. You can imagine our disappointment.

Sometimes, today's educational debates about length of school day and year remind me of that momentous change. A twelfth year was supposed to raise standards...just like longer days and year round schools. I hope they work.

This was also the year when West Charlotte High School was built on Beatties Ford Rd. (Now North West School of the Arts) and populated from the student body and instructors of Second Ward High School. Many of my classmates and teachers were transferred.

Mr. J. E. Grisby was Principal of Second Ward High School. His two pet sayings were: "Do and the world recognizes" and *"If you build the best rat trap in the world, the world will beat a path to your door. The* Negro *must build a better rat trap"*. There were 26 teachers, school secretary (Miss M. Taggart), school nurse (Mrs. B. H. Sansom) and a Librarian (Mr. D. B. Moore).

For your information, subjects taught at Second Ward were: English, Journalism, Arithmetic, Mathematics, Science, Chemistry, Physics, History, Geography, Economics, Latin, French, Home Economics (sewing & cooking), Manual Arts, Masonry, Music, Chorus, Band, Diversified Occupation Club (Dr. M. M. Adams, Coordinator) and Dramatics.

Extra curricular activities included football, basketball, the debate team and the junior-senior prom. Some clubs and organizations at Second Ward High School were: Democracy Club, Geographical Society, Girl Reserve, Safety Patrol, Herald Staff, Quill & Scroll, Dramatic Group, Diversified Occupation Club, Chorus and Band.

Special projects include: **Miss Second Ward,** who presides over the homecoming day. The election, conducted by the American Democracy Class, was patterned after the state and city elections, with registration days, filling of candidates, qualification of voters, and the election; the **May Queen**. A ballot was in the school newspaper, The Herald. A ballot was marked, cutout and placed in a sealed voting box. At a designated time, the votes were counted and the winners revealed. There was a crowning coronation, also dancers and flower girls. The **May Queen** reigned over activities for the day including wrapping the maypole.

The 1942 May Queen and Court were: Margaret Alexander (May Queen); Jennie Richardson (Maid-of-Honor); Helen Phillips, Inez Miller, Annie Mae Ivey-McPherson, Venus Smith, Bobbie Thompson and Ruby Coles.

Presently, I am blessed to be 89 years young. Unfortunate, I have lost track of Jennie Richardson, Venus Smith, Bobbie Thompson and Ruby Coles. However, Helen Phillips-Brooks and Inez Miller-Dixon are deceased. Currently, Annie Mae Ivey resides in Charlotte, NC. She's well and looks great.

It was thrilling, wonderful and truly an honor to be May Queen of Second Ward High School. It might not seem so exciting to someone today, but back then, it was a big deal Think homecoming and prom queen rolled into one. As long as memory lives, I'll always remember.

Little did I realize that in the year 2000, I would be looking at 16mm film footage of Second Ward High School, an all Black school in Charlotte, NC during segregation, in a documentary, "There Was A Colored School". It was produced and directed by Kathryn Frye. The Second Ward High School Film Project was produced by the Second Ward High School National Alumni Foundation, Inc. and the North Carolina Center for Educational Films. The documentary footage shows the detail of school days and various activities there in the 1940's and so much more. The film was a centerpiece of Black History month in February 2000.

I can visualize the safety-patrol girls and boys in their blue and white uniforms; classes marching out on the school grounds for fire drill once or twice a month; assembling in the auditorium for various activities (each class was assigned a section of the auditorium). The fenced-in playground was at the back of the school. The cafeteria was in the center basement. Social activity consisted of school parties and dances, the prom, social club dances by invitation only and birthday parties at home.

This was the time when anyone could buy a small bag full of candy for five cents, ride the bus or streetcar for seven cents, transfer for five cents; Taxi Cabs were ten cents. A five dollar pair of shoes was considered expensive, a beautiful felt hat could be purchased for ninety-eight cents in Belk basement and a three-quarter length topper coat sold for three dollars and ninety-eight cents.

BLACK and WHITE signs marked the water fountains downtown. No toilet facilities for African American shopper's downtown. Hotels, theaters, recreation facilities were not open to people of color. We met in churches and lodged in homes when various conferences and conventions came to town. Only one hospital was open for us, Good Samaritan Hospital. If you go down to the Bank of America Stadium, a historical marker indicates where "Good Sam" stood. Even the County Home was segregated.

The 2012 Republican National Convention in Tampa, Fla., was full of calls for a return to the "good old days". The conservatives never seem to understand that their "good old days" were days of repression, segregation, and second class citizenship for African Americans. Nostalgia for the days of white supremacy is not the smartest recruiting tool.

Throughout the years, I've frequently heard numerous positive comments regarding "There Was a Colored School". It is truly my privilege to be a 1942 graduate of Second Ward High School. There were many wonderful experiences at Second Ward. The curriculum consisted of basic courses, as well as, a multiplicity of extracurricular classes and activities. Upon graduation, we were prepared academically for college or the workforce. Also, we learned something about social graces, esthetics, the community and the government.

It was a time of social segregation and political suppression. Second Ward prepared us for the limited job opportunities a segregated South provided. But it did a bit more than that, within its hallowed halls our teachers tried to prepare our young minds for other possibilities. The world was at war and the growing demands of the defense plants were putting pressure on southern traditions. Black young men wanted to join the military and fight; others of us wanted to go into commerce or education. We didn't denigrate domestic service, but we wanted more.

There was a thirst for Knowledge and a desire to excel. We were inspired to move on to greatness. Students were very competitive in their schoolwork. Our playground, located behind the school, was fenced-in red clay where the team also practiced football. Football games were played at the Army Auditorium's Memorial Stadium. West Charlotte High School was our greatest rival. Students used hand-me-down uniforms and band instruments, second-hand books and used school equipment, a makeshift cafeteria in the school basement and a multi-purpose auditorium. We opened windows for fresh air. We learned to improvise or do our best with what we had. That spirit infused my generation, making us want what the white man had, whether in politics, housing or job security. We were not confrontational, or most of us weren't, but we knew that life could be better. We dreamed that one day, we too would get the new books, not the hand me downs.

Second Ward teachers showed great interest in the student body and aided in the progress of the school. They taught lessons of everyday life as well as academics. Home, school and church were the center of our universe. We looked forward to graduating from high school, going to college and graduating, securing a job and being successful in a chosen career, marriage, children, a comfortable, happy and secure family lifestyle. Segregated as those times were, we were mundanely middle class in our aspirations. Some of us realized those dreams. Unfortunately, others did not, I regret to say.

Humbly, I am sincerely appreciative and thankful for all the blessings bestowed upon me and mine. I've found that cherishing happy moments make a fine cushion for seasoned senior citizens. My children however don't want me to sit on the porch and just rock. They are constantly challenging me to think, to speak out, to read; to have opinions on the contemporary issues of the day. Kelly Jr. and I talk politics constantly, ranging from the civil rights movement to the latest on the morning news. Alfred, though the younger of my two sons, sometimes sounds more the seasoned political operative keeping his brother grounded in the practical of "getting it done."

Upon our graduation from Second Ward in 1942, West Charlotte's robes were late arriving; so our class was asked to let them use our robes. Now there was quite a bit of rivarey between the schools; so you know we were a bit upset. Nevertheless, the robes were used. I recall that Ruth Houser-Samuel wore my robe.

Our class officers were: Andrew Gray, President; Andrew played the xylophone and became a Certified Public Accountant, along the way he worked for many years with my husband at the funeral home; William Ezell, Vice President; Lunell Hart, Secretary; William Wells, Treasure.

Our motto was: "We Launch to Anchor Where"?

A stanza from Our Farewell Song: (Tune of "This Love of Mine") Words by: Helen Wise

Dear Second Ward, now we must go
We'll miss you always for we loved you so
You'll always be our guide all through life's storm
We'll always think of you, when things go wrong.

+++++++++++++++++

Chorus to our Class Song: (Tune of "Who Call") Words by Robert Alexander

Chorus

Farewell we hate to leave you all this way
Dear School we'll always think of you each day.
Farewell, tho we wish that we could stay
But in sadness we must say Farewell.

High School "First Love"

MY HIGH SCHOOL "boy friend" or "sweet heart" was Clarence "Duggie" Strong. Just about everybody, including us, thought we'd get married one day. However, that event was not to be. Nevertheless, we enjoyed each other's company while it lasted. As a matter of fact, the families involved remained close friends throughout their lives.

While I was home from college during spring break between my freshman and sophomore years, I met Kelly Alexander at Grace Loritts birthday party. Clarence was in the army over seas (World War II). Kelly and I became interested in each other and gradually fell in love.

Everything ended with Clarence and I breaking up. I returned his pictures and class ring.

Later, Clarence relocated to New York City; eventually married, produced two sons and subsequently died there.

Kelly and I married April 21, 1946 at 6:00 am, Easter Sunday morning.

Everlasten Love

M EETING KELLY M. Alexander, falling in love with him; a
year and four months engagement; marring him on Easter
Sunday morning at 6:00 am, April 21, 1946; was indeed a highlight
and turning point of my life.

When I think of our love story, I remember Cinderella and Prince
Charming or the "girl who lives on the other side of the railroad
tracks, who won the heart of the handsome prince". Also, I heard
the voice of my father's sister, Odessa Alexander Sloan McDowell,
whom I called Aunt Love, making comparisons of our marriage to
that of England's Queen Elizabeth and Prince Phillip. "Imagine
that!" I don't know what she was on at the time, but her mind was
indeed on overflow.

Never the less, I sincerely believe that Kelly and I were destined
to marry each other and be together, as the wedding vows say, "Until
death do us part", which is exactly what happened.

We always ended our love letters to each other with "I love you
forever and after." I am filled with so many wonderful and pleasant
memories of our life together.

Our wedding ceremony took place in my parent's living room with
my pastor Rev. Joseph F. Kendrick officiating. Today you would call
it a private ceremony. Only a few family and friends were present.
Afterwards, pictures were taken and breakfast served. My father-in-
law sent my new husband on a funeral; while I attended Mt. Moriah
Primitive Baptist Church's regular 11:00am church service. We saw

each other later that evening; went riding around the city and spent our first night together as man and wife at his family residence on South Caldwell Street. Four days later, on the following Wednesday, newlywed or not, it was back to college for me.

The private nature of our wedding, coupled with the brevity of our "honey moon" let some of the older sisters in the neighborhood to speculate on whether daddy had attended the nuptials with shotgun in hand. It was two years later that my first child arrived. From a 21st century perspective its no big deal, one way or the other, but back in 1946 arriving at the alter with a bun in the oven, bordered on the scandalous. Pregnant girls without marriage prospects disappeared from school were shipped off to relatives "out of state" or sequestered at home. Pregnant school teachers vanished from the class room. Things were known, but never talked about in polite society. So rumors were an assault on the virtue of the young lady in question. Especially hurtful in a time when premarital sex, though practiced, was frowned upon and condemned from the pulpit.

Kelly and my parents came to my graduation in May, 1946. From that point onward we were happily married until his death, April 2, 1985. My husband died on the couch in our family room, with me seated at his side. We had a grand life together. For a time I was stunned because he had been such an integral part of my life; I was emotionally adrift, thinking that my life was near an end. Thankfully, my sons didn't give up on me. They encouraged me to reengage, to get back out in to the world, to write about my life.

Returning to Charlotte after college graduation, I lived with my husband and his parents at 517 South Caldwell Street. It was the hardest thing to be in Charlotte and not see my parent's everyday but I had to adjust to doing just that. I had to learn a lot of things regarding married life. When I lived at home things were done for me, but as a wife I was expected to maintain the home; no servants a la Queen Elizabeth, just me, a pile of dirty clothes; a kitchen and soon the demands of two young boys. I was willing to learn because I wanted our marriage to be successful.

For a short period of time, I believe my husband was a bit sensitive regarding our age difference of nine years. I recollect attending a reception at the Episcopal Church Parish in Third Ward at which in going up the steps together, Mrs. Thomas Watkins asked my husband if I was his daughter (as a joke of course). We laugh and let it go at that.

On the other hand, I looked at the age difference as a plus because I preferred his maturity, insight and intelligence to that of the younger men I knew. I gain so much knowledge and wisdom from my husband. Through the years, we enjoyed the company of older friends. As the ole expression goes: "I'd rather be an older man's darling than a young man's fool". How about that? They got that right!

Since my husband was nine years my senior, quite naturally before our marriage, we socialized with different age level of friends and acquaintances. However, our paths crossed occasionally. Then too, I knew of the Alexander Funeral Home and heard of the Zechariah Alexander, Sr. family long before I became a member.

Later, we relocated to 415 East Stonewall Street. Momma Lou and Poppa were getting-on in age; therefore, it was more like they were living with us instead of the other way round. Nevertheless, we were there for each other as long as their life lasted. [2]

Kelly, Sr. and I produced two sons; Kelly, M., Jr. (October 17, 1948) and Alfred L. (November 10, 1952). They have made us proud; I'm blessed and pleased to report.

+++++++++++++++++

"Ghetto" is defined as a deprived quarter of a city in which members of a minority group are required to live, especially because of social, legal or economic pressure. I was born, reared and lived for at least twenty-one years in First Ward or "Cody Town" and in Second Ward or "Brooklyn" for sixteen years. I did not know or realize, until I heard the expression in high school, that First and Second Wards were designated as a "ghetto". That was quite a surprise, shock and awaking for me. I could not believe what I was hearing.

I have come to realize that much more than a physical place, a ghetto is a state of mind. If you believe that your physical surroundings define your prospects in life, then you have been truly placed into a cage from which you will never escape. My parents surrounded me with love; they made me believe that my surroundings contained endless possibilities and that though we were constrained by segregation and white supremacy, I could make my way in the world with dignity and grace. I have come to realize that they gave me the gift of believing in myself and that belief has helped sustain me all the years since.

I experienced a very happy childhood. My parents provided a very good lifestyle for me. They took excellent care of my needs and most of my wants. Momma and Daddy were always there for me. I am extremely appreciative, grateful and blessed to be their daughter. Momma died in 1976 and Daddy in 1984. Our love is always and forever.

My mother, Mrs. Alberta Wallace Alexander, who was known as "Bert" by her close friends and Momma by me, lived a life filled with helpfulness. She touched many lives with her good deeds. She was always willing to share what she possessed with those in need. She also represented a life of faithfulness. I'll always remember the worthwhile things she said and the useful things she did. My life is richer because of those precious memories.

My mother came from a generation, born during Reconstruction that lived to see both the rise of black power and its fall with the upsurge of white supremacy. Education was encouraged as a way to rise above agricultural toil, but Momma did not go very far in school. I was told that she and a girl friend, "Tug", fell prey to the pleasures of hanging out during school hours frequently playing hooky from school.

Momma regretted that decision immensely but she was smart enough not to dwell on the mistakes of her youth. Rather she pushed her daughter to do what she hadn't; to learn to read, write and count; to be prepared for a world different from hers. Momma went to night school for a while, tried reading my first & second grade books; she learned to write her name and was fortunate enough to be blessed with a good memory, eidetic they call it these days. For sure, she had no problem counting money. Many did not know or realize she was illiterate. Momma was a very good cook. The recipes were in her head. She was spick and span and wore her earbobs[10] and apron everyday. Everybody knew that she was "the boss of the house". She said what she meant and meant what she said.

Momma was one of the Mothers of Mt. Moriah Primitive Baptist Church; member, Sisterhood and Pastors Aid Club. Mothers were equivalent to female deacons. Momma was the oldest of her siblings: her brothers – James Clarence Wallace, John Ephraim Wallace, Walter "Sonny" Wallace; sister, Odessa Wallace Cloud, her Mother, my grandmother, Lula Conner Wallace (who died when I was in 5th grade). I remember standing by her bed fanning her before she died. All of my mother's siblings gravitated to her as a mother figure – maybe because she was the oldest. Momma and Aunt Odessa were inseparable, very close until her death. I was like the daughter who Aunt Odessa never had. The brothers visited Momma during the summer and keep in touch with letters. Sometime we visited them in New York City during my childhood.

To know with certainty how our moral compass has been set, we must understand our antecedents. My husband's father, Zechariah Alexander, Sr., was born in 1877, a turbulent time in the history of the American South; especially so for black people, because our Republican allies and benefactors settled a national election by abandoning us to the tender impulses of white supremacists. Rutherford B. Hayes becomes president; the federal troops were removed from the South; the bed sheets came out of the cupboards and the long march of Jim Crow began.

My father, Eulie L. G. Alexander, was born a few years after the Wilmington Riots overthrew a duly elected government putting the white supremacists of the Democratic Party firmly in control of North Carolina. It was September 5, 1902. The year before President Theodore Roosevelt shocked the South by inviting Booker T. Washington to have dinner at the White House.

James K. Vardaman of Mississippi reflecting supremacist opinion described the White House as "so saturated with the odor of the nigger that the rats have taken refuge in the stables". U. S. Senator Benjamin Tillman of South Carolina flatly stated, "The action of President Roosevelt in entertaining that nigger will necessitate our killing a thousand niggers in the South before they will learn their place again."

Both men, raised in the crucible of white oppression, tried to shield their children from the harsh realities of the time; imbuing my husband and I with a desire to be treated with the full rights of an American citizen. My husband's family was more overtly political, openly chafing at the social norms. One family followed the philosophy of W. E. B. Dubois, social integration and equal political rights, while the other was more in line with Booker T. Washington's, more gradualist approach. It was the black philosophical split of the time personified in two proudly American families that shared the same values of self-sufficiency, a belief in hard work and the conviction that education was the way forward for their children.

Politically aware or socially active blacks of my parents and father-n-laws generation were Republican in their thinking and voting. Southern Democratic politicians played the race card being completely white supremacist, supporting disfranchisement of black voters. It is ironic that by the 21st century it is the Republican Party that is the "white mans party", the champion of policies that are aimed at curtailing the votes of black people; while Democratic politicians are viewed as the champions of inclusiveness with the desire to have all citizens be active registered voters.

The memory of the 1898 Wilmington Race Riots was still very much alive within the black community during my father's formative years. On November 10 (coincidentally my youngest son's birthday), 1898, White Supremacists (mostly Democratic) took to the streets of Wilmington to overthrow the duly elected city government, made up of black and white Republicans and Populists. This "Fusion" politics was a threat to white supremacy and had to be stamped out at all costs. I wasn't until 2006, 108 years later, that a state commission finally recognized that the Wilmington Riots were acts of mob violence that the state in some way had to recognize as such and atone for.

My father, whom I call Daddy, had more formal education than Momma. He could read, write, was good in mathematics and was "a Jack of all trades". He was very good with his hands; constructing, building and driving. Daddy and Mr. Jim Ivey were entrepreneurs in Plastering, Cement Work and the Hauling business. He did lots of improvement work around our home. Daddy enjoyed gardening, raising pigeons, chickens, hogs and playing baseball. [11] He followed the worlds' series and read numerous books regarding the game and players. He was gentle, sincere, kind, devoted and dependable.

He accepted opportunities of service and used his time, energies and resources to help his fellowman. Daddy was an active member and deacon of Mt. Moriah Primitive Baptist Church[12]; Men's Bible Class of the Church Sunday School and member of the Committee for New Members class. He had the responsibility of preparing the bus list each year for members who were to attend the State Convention and the Senior Citizens Christmas Party. He formerly was the Assistant Superintendent of the Church Sunday School and also a Sunday School Teacher. He worked actively with the Boy Scouts.

He had the distinction of being the oldest father in the Church for 1982 and 1983. He was a member of the National Association for the Advancement of Colored People (NAACP) and served on the Board of Directors of Alexander Funeral Home Mutual Burial Association.

Daddy was eight years of age when his mother (Grandma Della Davis Alexander) died at age 41 in 1910. As the oldest child, he felt responsible for the well-being of his siblings, Odessa, age 7 and Cora, age 5, (my Aunt Love and Aunt Sis respectively) and acted accordingly with help from family and friends. Daddy really had to grow-up quickly, go to work sooner in order to help support his sisters until they could support themselves.

During my lifetime, I've spent lots of time visiting and talking with these two aunts. I did not have the pleasure of knowing my

Daddy's mother (Grandma Della) because I wasn't born until 1924. Unfortunately, I've never seen a picture of her. Back then they did not take many photographs. You may be sure; a photo of her would be greatly appreciated.

I grew-up playing with Aunt Sis's children. Also, I took our sons (Kelly, Jr. & Alfred) to visit her and their cousins, the Massey's and Burtons. Both aunts were very good cooks. Many days I enjoyed Aunt Sis's delicious tea cookies and sitting in her kitchen talking with her. Aunt Love and I sat in the swing on her front porch in the evening and talked frequently. I always enjoyed her delicious deserts and hamburgers with onion patties. When our sons were born, Aunt Love had married Willie McDowell. Currently, Uncle Willie's daughter, Annette Ardrey and his grand daughter, Sandra Ardrey and I are members of the Rosa M Morris Chapter No. 650, Order of the Eastern Star and the Queen City Chapter, National Women of Achievement, Inc. As a matter of fact, they usually drive by my house and take me with them to our meetings. They are what I call "good people" and wonderful friends, as well as kin.

Daddy died January 14, 1984 at his home, 421 East 21st Street in Charlotte, NC. I am truly grateful he was with me all those happy years. He was age 82 at his death.

At the time, I didn't think passing away at home was unusual. After all I had grown up in the era of intergenerational housing. Children often lived in households, with parents and grandparents. The old and young were intermingled in such a way, that births and deaths within a household were not remarkable.

+++++++++++++++++++

My first encounter with my father-in-law, Mr. Zechariah Alexander, Sr., affectionately called "Plain Z" and whom I called Poppa, was as a young girl about nine years of age playing softball in an alley-way between East 10th & East 11th Streets across from our home at 709 E. 11th St. He and his young son were walking from the direction of North Alexander Street. They greeted us as they walked down the alley way[13]. We were playing in a place where the alley way widened. Mr. Z. Alexander, Sr. was a distinguish elder gentleman of around 55 all decked out in his white suit and straw boater perhaps to visit a client to collect for or to write insurance. After all, he was District Manager of the Charlotte District of North Carolina Mutual Life Insurance Company[14] for approximately twenty-five years (beginning in 1902). Incidentally, the young man with him might have been his youngest son, Kelly Miller Alexander, then around 18, who just happens to be the man I married in 1946. His other sons were: Zechariah, Jr., Fred D. and Louis F. Alexander.

The second time I recollect seeing Kelly Alexander, Sr., I was approximately eleven or twelve years of age walking with friends, Inez and Willie Mae, going to the Lincoln Theater on East First Street. He and Tom Simmons[15] were standing on the front porch of Alexander Funeral Home, 323 South Brevard Street, and greeted us as we walked by.

Thirdly, I believe I saw a young Kelly with his mother visiting the Peeler family who lived on E. Eleven Street between N. Alexander and N. Davidson Streets, within a block from my home on E. Eleven St. I just happen to pass by on my way to Covington's grocery store located on the corner of E. Eleven and N. Caldwell Streets.

The adults were seated on the front porch while the young folk were playing in the fenced-in front yard. The Peelers also owned a small one or two room house next to their home where young people from their church came to teach Bible study to the neighborhood children. The Peelers and Kelly's mother were members of Seven Street Presbyterian Church.

In hind sight, I remember also whenever I visited the Clarence Strong Sr. family who lived about three houses from the Zechariah Alexander, Sr. family home on South Caldwell Street, between East First & E. Stonewall Streets, I never saw Kelly but I'm sure he saw me at some point.

On another occasion after the "May Queen" celebration activities, when I was about seventeen or eighteen, Kelly came to Second Ward High School to Principal Grisby's office to inquire about a photograph of the May Queen Court . He was a reporter and salesman for the Afro-American [16]Newspaper, and wanted the photograph to go into the next edition of the paper. The office sent Kelly to contact me in Journalism class regarding the picture. With my parents' consent, Kelly drove me home to get the photograph and immediately back to school. He was polite, very professional, respectful and a gentleman.

Our next meeting was at Grace Loritts-Stevenson's Birthday party on Baldwin Avenue in the Cherry Section of Charlotte. It was 1944, the summer between my freshman and sophomore year in college, when Grace came to First Ward to invite Inez, Nannie, Willie Mae and I to her party. She mentioned that Kelly had asked if I was invited. She told him yes. That is the first time I knew he had noticed me and had an interest.

My girlfriends and I went to the party; in walks Kelly with a girl from New York City, who was visiting relatives in Charlotte. My girlfriends and I looked at each other with surprised expressions. I must admit a sinking feeling of disappointment. However, Kelly took the young lady home early; came back to the party; monopolized the remainder of the evening talking and dancing with me. He drove me and my friend's home after the party.

Frequent telephone calls and site-seeing throughout the city followed. Our interest in each other grew during the rest of the summer before I left for college in Durham, NC. About the same time he left Charlotte to attend Renourd College of Embalming in New York City. We exchanged letters. I still have a shoebox full of the letters he wrote to me while I was in college. I sometime wonder how the internet generation will preserve their memories since they text, instant message and email. Electronic files are so 21st century, but nothing beats my box of good old fashioned paper letters.

After one year and six months, we became engaged to each other on Christmas Eve 1944. Kelly had bought my engagement ring in New York. It was gift wrapped in a very large box; inside that box was another wrapped medium size box and another smaller wrapped box until my beautiful platinum diamond engagement ring was revealed. Just the right size too! My mouth was wide open with joy. Kelly proposed. I accepted without hesitation. That evening he asked my parents for their permission and blessings to marry. We discussed the matter and promised we'd wait until I finished college before getting married. My education was of uttermost importance to my parents and making sure that this is what I really wanted to do at that point in my life. All were in agreement.

My wedding band was purchased in Charlotte, NC. I gave Kelly a gold wedding band. Presently, my wedding band and engagement ring are worn on a silver chain around my neck. Due to a little arthritis in the joints of my fingers.

In 1985 after my parents, husband, and in-laws died, I had two rings made (a dinner ring and a ring for my little finger) with the gold and stones from my mother's wedding ring, my husband's wedding band, Momma Lou's broach and Poppa's stick pen. These rings are now worn on a gold chain. Poppa enjoyed walking. He did not drive at all. Every evening he'd walk to the Post Office downtown on West Trade Street (now the Federal Court Building). As a matter of fact, he was out walking one evening when he was hit by a car that caused his death in 1954 at age 77.

Mr. Zechariah Alexander, Sr. attended Myers Street School and the Normal school of Biddle University, now Johnson C. Smith University, which he finished in 1896.

During his early life, he worked in building trade as a lathing contractor; bookkeeper for the W.W. Houser Brick Company. During the Spanish American War (1898)[17] he served in the Army, as a Regimental Sergeant Major, 3rd Regiment, NC Colored Volunteers, USA. In 1902, he was attracted to the insurance business and served as District Manager of the Charlotte District of the North Carolina Mutual Life Insurance Company for approximately 25 years. After retiring from the insurance business, he devoted his full time to the Funeral Service business which he operated in partnership with his sons.

He was a member of Friendship Missionary Baptist Church;

served on the Board of Management of the H.L. McCrorey branch Y.M.C.A.; and was associated with most of the movements for the advancement and improvement of Negro life in the community. He served as Deputy Imperial Potentate of the Ancient Egyptian Arabic Order, Nobles of the Mystic Shrine, and the honor of Imperial Potentate Emeritus was conferred upon him at the 1954 Imperial Council Session held in Atlantic City, N.J. He served as Chairman of the Committee of Foreign Correspondence of the Most Worshipful Prince Hall Grand Lodge F. & A. Masons, Jurisdiction of North Carolina. He was an active member of the United Supreme Council 33rd Degree of the Ancient and Accepted Scottish Rite of Freemasonry, Southern Jurisdiction. He was a member of Knights of Pythias, Elks; and Past Master of Unique Lodge No. 85, Prince Hall Masons.

First Meeting with Kelly, Sr.'s Mother

WHILE KELLY, SR. was in New York City attending Renouard College of Embalming, he had asked me to visit his mother in order for us to get to know each other better. We spent about two or three hours together that evening talking and enjoying delicious chicken salad, potato chips, cheese straws, hot Russian tea and cookies. The meeting went well for both of us.

Kelly arranged for an employee at Alexander Funeral Home, Inc. to drive me to and from their home to mine.[18] I found Mrs. Louise Alexander to be very pleasant and hospitable. I must admit, I was a bit nervous upon arrival. But Momma Lou's demeanor calmed my nervousness. If that first meeting was a test, evidently, I passed, because, on December 24th of that year, Kelly surprised me with an engagement ring and a proposal of marriage. Of course, I willingly accepted both.

We've all heard lots of Mother-in-law jokes. Seemingly, they or we get a raw deal most of the time. Anyway, I am pleased to report that my Mother-in-law, Mrs. Louise Beatrice McCullough Alexander, who I called "Momma Lou", was great (a warm gentle lady).

Momma Lou attended Myers Street School and Scotia Seminary in Concord, North Carolina. Early in life she joined Seventh Street Presbyterian Church in Charlotte, NC and was a devoted member until her death, November 10, 1955 at age 77. Momma Lue was a Christian mother and devoted her entire life to her family, who put the motto: "Christ is Head of this house; the Unseen Guest at every meal; the Silent Listener to every conversation." always before them. She taught her family Obedience, Love, Reverence, Patience, Forbearance; considering these household virtues.

She had a Christian courage. It was not a factor with her what others did; she had the courage to do what she thought was right. Her conduct had gone beyond the point of being swayed by what was popular or customary. She had further, the culture of unselfishness which lost itself in service to others. She suffered least from her own pains and most from the sorrows of others.

She was a member of the Southside Art and Literary Cub; Golden Hue Chapter No. 15, Order of the Eastern Star; Rameses Court No. 78, Daughter of Isis; Circle No. 4, Women's Missionary Society and the Deaconess Board of Seventh Street Presbyterian Church.

+++++++++++++++++++

Upon returning to Charlotte, NC after my college graduation, Poppa and Momma Lou were in the process of selling their home on South Caldwell Street and relocating to their family home at 415 East Stonewall Street (which was previously rented and was now being upgraded for us to move into); a two story, twenty-three room, home on S. Caldwell St. By today's standards is much too large a place, but made sense in a time when multiple generations might live under the same roof.

Early on, Momma Lou operated a "boarding house" for out-of-town public school teachers. When Kelly and I married in 1946, a portion of the house was not in use. Momma Lou and Poppa stayed with Zack, Jr. and Mildred Alexander while we waited for the house on East Stonewall St. to be refurbished.

Meanwhile, Kelly and I kept house for Dorothy and Alfred Flag on South Fox Street in the Cherry neighborhood, while they were in Orangeburg, South Carolina for a summer school break. After our stay there, we moved in with Ruth and Charles Gilliard on the corner of East 9th and North Alexander Street in the First Ward neighborhood. I am pleased to say that I learned quite-a-bit from these two ladies because both were home-economics teachers. Ruth also served as principal of a small county school. I do not remember the name of the school or its location. There were only two teachers. One classroom for First, Second and Third grades and one classroom for Fourth, Fifth and Sixth grades. Each grade was separated by rows. I recall being a substitute teacher there when Ruth's mother died. Ruth was unable to secure one of her regular substitute teachers at the time.

Kelly, Sr., our sons', Kelly, Jr. & Alfred and I lived with his parents after we married until they died. We had planned to build and have them live with us; but both of his parents died before our plans materialized in 1962. Urban Renewal moved us and many more out of Second Ward.

As a young inexperienced wife and mother, I gained much constructive knowledge and wisdom from my husbands' parents.

Momma Lou taught me how to cook; helped immensely with our sons when they were born and while they were growing up. We sat on the front porch in the evenings at 415 E. Stonewall St. and talked about life experiences, dreams and expectations. Quiet often, Poppa was traveling on Masonic business and my husband on NAACP business.

When Momma Lou gave me Kelly, Sr.'s pajamas and underwear to launder the first time, I asked "What do you want me to do with these clothes?" She replied, "Do anything you want to do with them. They belong to you now. You can either wash them or have them laundered." I suppose she was glad to pass them on to me. Then she said, "If you prefer washing them, you can use the washing machine." I asked her to show me how to operate the machine and proceeded to wash the items from then-on.

My husband told me years later that his mother asked him, "Where did you get this girl? She doesn't know how to do anything." Kelly, Sr. asked her to be patient with me and teach me because I really did not know what was expected of me to do at this point.

That was indeed a true fact. I was willing and anxious to learn because I wanted to have a successful married life. I was not a visitor or guest anymore, but indeed a member of the family. Now they tell me that I turned out to be a pretty good wife, mother, cook, secretary and hostess.

Momma Lou was instrumental in reminding me to be hospitable toward company intermittently stopping by the house to visit. "It's gracious to offer some type of refreshment. It could be food or beverage: i.e. tea, coffee or punch; cheese & crackers; cake, cookies; potato chips, cheese straws; a salad: potato, chicken, congealed flavored plain or with fruit or vegetables with mayonnaise and a red cherry on top to make it appealing; spam, spice or boil ham.", She would say. "If you do not have on hand what you need in a situation like this and I do, use mine off the shelf. It can be replaced later." She shared her knowledge, experience and formidable pantry. From her, I learned just how important food was as an ice breaker and integral part of Southern hospitality.

Momma Lou and Poppa were like "two peas in a pod" who loved and cared deeply for each other. Everyone could literally see the devotion they had for each other.

Although, we (Kelly, Sr., Kelly, Jr., Alfred & I) were living with my Mother and Father-in-law in their home for several years, it was like our own home. Kelly, Sr.'s parents had reached an age where they were quite comfortable and happy with us "being in charge" or "running the show". It worked out fine for everybody. We were "One large happy family".

Also, in living with Momma Lou and Poppa, I was able to see and interact with numerous family members who visited. Some dropped in every year, like my brother in law, Louie Alexander and his wife, Maude, spending vacation time back in the South. Other friends and family just visited whenever they wanted to. They came from New York, New Jersey, Washington, D.C., West Virginia, Maryland, California, Raleigh, NC, Fayetteville, NC, and South Carolina. Because both Poppa and my husband were active in the civic life of the community, you simply never could predict when a visitor would knock on our door.

Helen Anthony Alexander

I AM FORTUNATE TO have been blessed with a lovely, wonderful and beautiful daughter-in-law, Helen Anthony Alexander, my youngest son, Alfred's wife. Helen is like my very own daughter. Often when we are out together, people mistakenly think that I am her mother. We usually do not tell them anything differently because of our mutual feelings of respect and love for each other.

Helen and I go shopping and on trips together, sharing a hotel room when need-be. She occasionally accompanies me to my various medical appointments. It's not unusual for Helen to take her mother, Mrs. DelMarie Anthony, and I to the Podiatrist for our appointments; followed by some treat or another, like lunch at the Cracker Barrel.

Both of us are members of the Queen City Chapter, National Women of Achievement, Inc.; Rosa M. Morris Chapter, No. 650, Order of the Eastern Star; and the Zack Alexander Assembly No. 35, Order of the Golden Circle. Helen is a past First Vice President, National Women of Achievement, Inc; both, she and Alfred are Deacons at Saint Paul Missionary Baptist Church where Rev. Gregory Moss is pastor. Recently, Helen was elected Loyal Lady Ruler of Zack Alexander Assembly No. 35, Order of the Golden Circle.

In 2009, when I was hospitalized and received a pacemaker, Helen stayed overnight with me. I stayed with her and Alfred at their home for two weeks recuperating. I thoroughly enjoyed my stay there with such good care. I felt so welcome and they assured me that their door was open to me always. Although it seemed like a vacation, I knew it was time to get off the cloud and face reality at home.

The family has developed an annual ritual; Helen and Alfred always prepare Thanksgiving dinner inviting friends and extended family to their home for a large event. Kelly, Jr. and I usually host a smaller family Christmas dinner. Every July 3, Helen and Alfred celebrate "July 4th" with a large cookout.

The ebb and flow of family ritual encompasses other branches of our blended families. Helen invites Kelly, Jr. and I to the "Anthony-Hough Family Reunion" and, of course, she attends the "Burton-Massey & Alexander Family Reunion".

One day last summer, Out-of-the-blue, Alfred, on his way to work came by Senior Drive to bring me a bag of goodies from Helen; fresh red cherries, a banana, fresh blue berries, peaches, a bag of glazed walnuts, a bag of Milano Milk Chocolate cookies and six Cinnamon bars. Delicious "nick-knacks [12] all day. Call it a random act of kindness, indicative of what holds our family together.

I could go on and on regarding Helen's caring attitude, but I'll stop here. I'm sure you get the drift. She's a jewel! I, too in numerous ways, show Helen my appreciation and love.

Alpha Kappa Alpha Sorority

H AVING KNOWN PERSONALLY individuals who were members of Alpha Kappa Alpha Sorority, I became involved in the Ivy Leaf Club as a freshman at North Carolina College for Negroes in 1943. I was inducted into the Alpha Chi Chapter of Alpha Kappa Alpha Sorority in 1945. It was one of the most important decisions of my life. The sorority not only brought friendships that lasted a lifetime, but it demanded that I stay academically focused. Being an AKA Soror motivated and stimulated me to work hard academically because I did not want to discredit the group in any form or fashion. We sisters bonded together for the good of the whole sorority. We were striving to be "the best" in whatever task we undertook.

I joined Alpha Lambda Omega Chapter of Alpha Kappa Sorority in 1946, after graduating from college. Today, I am a Golden Soror and a Life Member of Alpha Kappa Alpha Sorority.

My sister-in-law, Soror Mildred McCullough Alexander, wife of Zechariah Alexander, Jr. (my husband's brother) was a charter member of Alpha Lambda Omega Chapter, AKA Sorority, Inc.

Alpha Kappa Alpha Sorority, Incorporated organized in 1908 and is the oldest Greek-letter organization established by and for Black women. The Sorority was incorporated in 1913. Through the years, Alpha Lambda Omega has contributed financially to the support of the Charlotte-Mecklenburg County NAACP Branch and to other worthwhile organizations, institutions and causes. Implemented a Leadership Development Program for high school students in the Charlotte-Mecklenburg area. Does volunteer work in the community with various charities. Sponsor public political forums and collaborate with other organizations in voter registration and health fairs. Provide support base for minority students to compliment formal educational training.

To me, being selected "Scrollers' Sweetheart" in 1944 was indeed an honor, which I was delighted to accept.

While attending college, I was a member of the Commercial Club, Choir,

Sunday School, AKA Sorority and Year book Staff. I lived in Rush Hall as a freshman, Annie Day Shephard Dormitory (sophomore) and McLean Dormitory (Junior and senior years).

The rules were very strict. We had to sign out when leaving campus and sign in upon returning. Dormitories were either all male or all female. Male students were not allowed in the female student's room. Visitation was in the parlor. Only senior students were permitted to go off campus alone. All the other students were required to recruit two additional students to accompany them off campus. Parent's permission was required for a trip home or to travel elsewhere while enrolled on campus. Dormitory doors were locked every evening at a specific time. Vesper on Sunday and chapel was every Monday and Friday. Seats were assigned alphabetically. With my name, Alexander, I was always down front on the first row. Someone was in the balcony looking and marking present or absent for each seat in the auditorium. At this point, I do not remember the exact number of absentees permitted before a penalty took place.

Margaret Hickman was my roommate in college for three years. We were good friends and stayed in touch with each other until she died on August 1, 2009. She married the love of her life, James Evans in 1949 and they produced eleven children, James, Jr., Gregory, Dianne, Alicia, Cecilia, Angelia, Michelle, Samuel, Anthony, Gerard and Ruth; twenty-five grandchildren and fourteen great-grandchildren. Upon her graduation from North Carolina College for Negroes in 1946, she worked briefly at Fayetteville State Teachers College in Fayetteville, N.C. She was born in Boardman, N.C. and moved after marriage to Detroit. MI.

Today, as a seasoned senior citizen, I am pleased to still have and frequently wear the elegant gold square-face watch my husband, Kelly, Sr., gave me upon my graduation from college in 1946. Often, I wear the watch on Sundays or special occasions.

+++++++++++++++++++

There are two incidents of which I recall that were not all peaches and cream where I was concerned and they are:

The first incidence happen when I was an eighth grader on my way to Second Ward High School. A group joined in the walk there. I could hear some of the girls walking behind me chanting over and over, "There goes the black Queen". I acted as if I did not hear what they were saying.

This was long before I was selected "May Queen" in the eleventh and twelfth grades. I kept quite and walked on up the hill; but this was mean spirited harassing and humiliating. I told Mrs. Carson, my homeroom teacher who was also my "Play Mother", about the incident. She told me to, "hold my head up and ignore them." That is exactly what I did and the harassment soon stopped.

The second incident involved a group of us gathered at the home of our teacher, Miss Stevenson, after school one day; on my way out the door leaving her home, a male student lunged toward me with a sharp pencil directed at my face. Lucky for me that he missed damaging my eyes or face.

I reported this to my parents. Incidentally, this was the same individual who previously had shot a classmate in the eye with a sling-shot. He lived in First Ward. My parents immediately went to his home and discussed the matter with the male student's parents. He never bothered me again, I'm pleased to report.

Beds and Clothes Closet

As a young girl, I slept in my parent's bedroom in a single bed. Later as a teenager, my own furnished bedroom was provided for me by my parents. I recall the beautiful Hollywood bed, vanity with bench and chest of drawers. There was also a small clothes closet in the room. The bathroom equipped with bathtub, sink, stool and a mirrored door medicine cabinet on the wall, was immediately off my bedroom. Everything was so convenient; I really enjoyed and appreciated my very own bedroom. What a wonderful thoughtful gift to give your child!

In college, I slept in a single bed in three different dormitories. There were: two persons in one room; including two beds, two chairs, and one table with useable opening on both sides and two clothes closets. I recall taking a wooden orange crate, standing it upright and covering it with pink chintz material and using it as a storage table for food items (i.e., potted meat, sardines, peanut butter, and cream cheese with pineapple, Velveeta cheese, crackers, cookies, fruit cocktail and jello). A friend and classmate, Hattie Plummer Jones was a home economic student would make the jello for Margaret Hickman Evans, my roommate and I. We'd get cold drinks from the store and set them in the window to keep cool. Students did not have a refrigerator in their room while I was in college. On both ends of the hallway on each floor of the dorm, there was a large bathroom equipped to accommodate ten people at once.

After marriage, my husband and I slept together in a double bed.

In 1962, we purchased a king size bedroom suite. I always slept on the left side of our bed. Even after my husband died in 1985, I continued sleeping on the left side of our bed. The only time I would sleep on the right side of the bed was when I was ill. You see, the right side is closer to the telephone and the bathroom. In 2011, I purchased a queen size bedroom suite. Presently, I enjoy sleeping on my back, in the middle of my queen size bed. I must admit, it's quite comfortable and there's more walking space in the room.

Back in the day, there were few clothes closets in homes. That is why in 1962, when we built our home on Senior Drive, I requested a complete wall of closet space in each of the three bedrooms, a closet and storage space in the den and a hall closet near the foyer. Also we invested in a storage facility in the backyard.

A piece of furniture known as a wardrobe was used to store various apparel and to hang garments in to compensate for lack of closet space. As a matter of fact, I gave my parent's wardrobe and their long tall living room table to my son, Alfred. The wardrobe now holds a place of honor in his home office.

All this reminiscing has me thinking about linen and crochet doilies on sofa backs and chair arms, vanities and tables; plastic coverings on furniture and lamp shades to keep dust off. What a fire hazard? Someone up stairs was truly taking care of us, for sure!

Why am I talking about Beds and Closets? I don't know; just thought it would be interesting to write about while reflecting.

Catalog Shopping

CURRENTLY, I'M DOING quit a bit of catalog shopping leisurely at home instead of going to various malls, shops or department stores. Since I do not drive, it's convenient for me. So far, so good! My first foray in catalogue shopping was with colorful muumuus to wear mostly around the house or out casually. In cool weather, I wear a long sleeved tee shirt or top under the muumuu. They are comfortable, can be dressed up or down, easy to launder, look good and are inexpensive. I'm comfortable shopping from catalogues, but not online. There is just something about online shopping that I don't trust. Possibly all the stealing of credit card information that I see reported in the news.

After gaining confidence in catalogues, I moved on to purchasing skirts, tops, tees, crochet cardigans, cotton jackets, reversible dresses.

It's really fun mixing and matching two or three tops with one skirt for a different look. Then using various accessories to coordinate with each outfit. I frequently use my mother's earbobs and beads because now that jewelry is back in style. Otherwise, I select items from my own closet to enhance the new clothing. I really enjoy wearing these catalog purchased items and have receive numerous compliments when wearing them.

Home Sweet Home

T HUS FAR, I'VE lived in the following permanent homes. First with my parents, Eulie Lester Gilreece Alexander and Alberta Wallace Alexander, at 709 East Eleventh Street, Charlotte, North Carolina (located between North Alexander and North Myers Streets) - First Ward.

In 1946, Kelly and I lived with his parents, Zechariah and Louise Alexander at 517 South Caldwell Street, Charlotte, N.C. (Located between East First and East Stonewall Streets). This huge two story house had been used previously as a Boarding House. Mainly, public School Teachers who came from out of town. However, in 1946, the back portion of the house was not in use. Only the front up and down space was used and occupied by us.

From there, all of us moved to 415 East Stonewall Street (located between South Brevard and South Caldwell Streets). Now this is where Kelly and I started our family. (October 17, 1948 – Kelly Miller Alexander, Jr. and November 10, 1952 – Alfred Louis Alexander). This section of Charlotte is called "Second Ward" by some and "Brooklyn" by others.

Our home on East Stonewall Street consisted of: 2-living rooms, 1- dinning room, 1- Kitchen, 4- Bed rooms, 2- large hallways, only 1 – bathroom, 1- large screen –in front porch, 1- small back porch and ample space in the front and back yards.

Upon the death of Poppa and Momma Lou, Urban Renewal

came to the area. We then purchased two lots on Senior Drive in West Charlotte and built our current home in 1962.

My final resting place on earth is reserved at York Memorial in a space next to my beloved husband. Only the date is unknown. I strive every day to live by Christian principles that will one day permit me to make heaven my home.

Family Dogs

I'VE ALWAYS HEARD the expression, "A man's best friend is his dog". Somehow, I find that I prefer a dog as a pet rather than a cat.

The first dog in our family, while I was a young child, was Butch. He was black with white blotches. A real mutt, but I loved him.

My dog was Ranger, a brown and black curly hair of unknown lineage. He usually followed me to elementary school.

Kelly, Sr.'s dog was a brown cocker spaniel called Brownie. I met her while Kelly, Sr. and I were courting. Brownie was very jealous. When we sat beside each other on the sofa in the living room, Brownie would place her head between us and look sadly directly at us in order to get our attention.

Kelly, Jr.'s dog was a brown and white Cocker Spaniel named Freckles. At this time, Kelly, Jr. was our only child.

From high school through college, Alfred and Kelly, Jr. had two Siberian Huskies, Poncho and Cisco. Kelly, Sr. and I cared for them while our son's were attending North Carolina Central University in Durham, NC and the University of North Carolina at Chapel Hill. Siberian husky's love to dig holes and jump-up on you or pull you. I had a special trench coat to put over my clothes when I fed them in their fenced-in area of our back yard.

Kelly, Jr. wants us to get another dog, but he travels so much, that I'm afraid that I would soon become the defacto caregiver. At my age, I just don't want the responsibility. House dog you say. No any canine that joins the Alexander family will be living outside, with perhaps occasional house privileges. Alfred Louis, my youngest son feels the dog might make an awkward move and I may fall while I'm home alone, that's not good.

Living In Brooklyn &
The Impact of Friendship
Missionary Baptist Church

I WAS TWENTY-EIGHT YEARS of age; pregnant caring my son, Alfred, when I joined Friendship Missionary Baptist Church by Christian Experience in 1952. Rev. Coleman W. Kerry, Jr. was Pastor. Rev. Kerry's wife, Mariezetta, had been a Second ward High School classmate before West Charlotte High School was built on Beatties Ford Road. Her home was on the west side of the city therefore she had to transfer.

I literally grew-up in Mt. Moriah Primitive Baptist Church, which I joined at age twelve.

Kelly, Sr. and I married April 21, 1946. He, his brothers & father were members of Friendship Missionary Baptist Church. During this time, I frequently visited the church. My husband's father, Zechariah Alexander Sr., was Friendship's Sunday school 3rd Superintendent. He enrolled our sons in Friendship Cradle Role Class at birth. Sister Anita Stroud was their first Sunday school teacher.

We lived only one block from Friendship. Our home, 415 E. Stonewall St., was located between South Brevard & South Caldwell

Streets. Friendship was on the corner of South Brevard and East First Streets.

I am thankful to report that Friendship played a significant part in my spiritual and social life. I was a very active member for many years.

I worked diligently in the Missionary Circle when Sis. Pearl Cooper was President; and later with Sis. Daisy Coleman & Sis. Gulia Hatten-Mobley.

Individual Circles met in homes and all circles came together at a designated time at the church. I was a member of the Sheepfold of Bartholomew; twice chaired the Women's Day Program and was a member of the Woman's Day Committee for several years.

I also wrote and directed plays for Women's Day; typed stencils and ran-off programs for Revival; served as substitute Teacher for Sis. Minnie Banners Sunday school Class. Narrated "The Feast of Belshazzar" directed by Sis. Beulah John Perrin. Attended and presented at Workshops. Was one of the Advisors of the Friendship Junior NAACP Youth Council, (1959 – 1960's). Delegate to ABCOTT several times during the 1990's.

I usually traveled and roomed with Sister Artie C. Phillips. Sometime we rode with Sister Doretha L. Leake, Rev. J. R. Covington and Rev. Paxton Hughes. I became "A Diamond of Friendship Missionary Baptist Church", August 15, 2010.

Our current Pastor is Rev. Dr. Clifford A. Jones, Sr. who became the thirteenth pastor of Friendship Missionary Baptist Church in October, 1982. Our First Lady is Sister C. Brenda Reynolds Jones. Their daughter and son are now Rev. Michelle Jones and Rev. Anthony Jones. We are truly blessed and fortunate to have Dr. Clifford A. Jones, Sr. as our Pastor and Sister C. Brenda R. Jones as his helpmate. They complement each other and work well together for the betterment of our church family.

Friendship Missionary Baptist Church is an intricate part of my life. It is a secure place to worship and to fellowship with one another. We are educated, inspired, guided and motivated there. It helps keep us focused and revitalize the sprit within us to move forward in our daily Christian service to all mankind.

I am reminded to increase my faith, to strengthen my hope, deepen my love for everyone and to be humble, grateful and thankful for all the wonderful things God does and has done for us. We celebrate the birth of Jesus Christ and thank Him for giving us a chance to live a better life while traveling on this journey to make Heaven our eternal home. God has truly blessed me and I am indeed thankful to be in the land of the living today.

As I looked for something in my file yesterday, I came across a typed sheet of paper entitle "A MOMENT OF HISTORY". Its author is unknown I believe it was written for a program of senior citizens and mothers of Friendship Baptist Church. It reads as follows:

> *"The ages of the founding members of this church are not known. Many would think that they were elderly, inasmuch as they separated from another church due to dissension within the congregation and their wish not to get involved with this. Certainly they were people of courage, ideals, and high spiritual values. They were eager to "be about God's business!"*

Tom Thumb Wedding

THE TOM THUMB Wedding is a fictional wedding in which children participate as adults would in an actual wedding ceremony. The characters are: Bride, Groom, Maid of Honor, Best Man, Bride Maids, Groom's Men, Flower Girl, Ring Bearer, Preacher, Mother and Father of the Bride, Mother and Father of the Groom and Ushers. One or two solos and music before and after the event. The Preacher is really the star of the production, the ceremony is comical

Basically this is a fundraiser for some worthwhile organization. There's a reception after the program for all in attendance. The female and male raising the highest amount of money become the bride and groom.

Our sons, Kelly, Jr. and Alfred Louis participated in two Tom Thumb Weddings. One was sponsored by the Rosa M. Morris Chapter No. 650, Order of the Eastern Star and the other was sponsored by the Friendship Junior Youth Council, National Association for the Advancement of Colored People. I was the Director of both. They were very good fundraisers for each group.

Meeting Dr. Martin Luther King, Jr.

T HE CHARLOTTE-MECKLENBURG COUNTY Branch, National Association for the Advancement of Colored People (NAACP) invited Dr. Martin Luther King, Jr. to be guest speaker for a public meeting in Charlotte, North Carolina.

Dr. King, Jr. was unable to appear because of his being stabbed in New York City. Therefore, Rev. Ralph Abernathy came as a replacement. However, the following year, Dr. King, Jr. was invited by my husband, who was President of the North Carolina State Conference of Branches, National Association for the Advancement of Colored People, to be Guest Speaker in Charlotte, NC. Sponsored by the local NAACP branch at the Charlotte Park Center.

The crowd overflowed Park Center. Our sons, Kelly, Jr. and Alfred Louis, hung-out with their father that day. I rode to and from the event with our Pastor, Rev. Coleman W. Kerry, Jr. and his wife. Mrs. Kerry and I were high school classmates. Pastor Kerry, Jr. and Dr. King, Jr. attended Morehouse. Kelly, Sr. asked Pastor Kerry, Jr. to transport Dr. King, Jr. to the reception held at the Alexander Hotel (located at the corner of N. McDowell and E. 9th Streets (formerly, the Florence Crittenden Home where white parents sent their pregnant daughters to live and give birth to their babies).

At this time, there was not a Florence Crittenden Service Center for pregnant Afro Americans. They were usually either secluded behind closed doors at home, sent to visit a relative in another part of the city or state for at least a year, or to have an abortion. Those were the options. Some churches held a special meeting regarding the problem and ended up discharging the unwed pregnant female. Society looked down on young ladies in this particular situation.

In my childhood, I do not remember seeing a pregnant school teacher. A pregnant individual could not attend public school or an institution of higher learning during the 1930's and 1940's. Fortunately, today circumstances and ideas have changed for the betterment of all concerned.

This is when I met Dr. Martin Luther King, Jr. for the first time. Mrs. Kerry and I were in the back seat of the car and Dr. King, Jr. was in front with Pastor Kerry, Jr. driving. I found Dr. King, Jr. to be pleasant, amicable and polite; a perfect gentleman. He was introduced to us, was very complementary and conversed mostly with Pastor Kerry on our way to the reception. We did not stay for the reception because there was an evening Sunday service at Friendship and I returned home.

An interesting quotation from Martin Luther King, Jr. is: "Death is not a period at the end of the sentence of life … but a comma, punctuating it and lifting it to higher heights."

Christmas

MANY YEARS AGO, while growing up, seemingly the weather was cold in December. Sometimes there were even a few days of snow during the winter months. However, now it feels almost like spring or summer in December. The winter of 2013-2014 seems to be an exception, harkening back to the winters of the 40's and 50's.

As a child I enjoyed the Christmas Holiday Season. The beautiful music, singing carols, decorating the Christmas tree, Santa Clause, toys, games, gifts, presents and family Christmas dinner. As a teenager, I remember roller skating quite a bit during the Christmas Holiday Season.

There were two dolls in my childhood which I well remember Santa Clause bringing: One was a small infant baby doll with dark painted hair. Her dress was white with red dots all over it. The other was a larger baby doll with long curly hair. Her dress was a lovely light pink with white lace around the collar. She also had on white shoes and socks. I recall Santa Clause always left a shoe box filled with fruits, candy and assorted nuts and raisins under our tree in the living room.

Momma made several cakes to serve friends or guest visiting: Coconut, Carmel, Chocolate, Jelly and Pound or Plain cake. The Fruit Cake was purchased. Momma did not have an electric mixer; therefore, she used a large bowl, egg-beater and a large spoon to mix the ingredients. Most of the cakes were layers baked in tin pie pans. I was always ready to taste the small sample of cake which Momma baked first. This was in order to determine whether everything was satisfactorily done. Momma did not use a recipe; measurements and ingredients were all in her head. However, I am here to tell you that she was a wonderfully excellent baker. My sons, Kelly, Jr. and Alfred ate her biscuits without butter, jam or meat and enjoyed every bite. Her biscuits were nice and soft days after they were baked. I never did manage Momma's technique. Later in life, she told me that I didn't use enough shortening in my biscuits. I'm thinking that maybe it was the buttermilk too because sometime I used sweet milk instead.

As an adult married lady, after perfecting my cooking, Kelly, Sr. and I usually hosted the family Christmas Dinner which included nineteen individuals. At this time Kelly, Jr. and I have cut the Christmas list down considerably. All that cooking is hard work.

We always had a live tree which Kelly, Sr., Kelly, Jr., Alfred Louis and I decorated. Electric candles were placed in the windows at 415 E. Stonewall Street and Christmas greeting cards were attached to ribbon and draped around the archway and doorways of the living rooms. A pot or two of pinsetters were placed somewhere in the area.

It was lots of work preparing the meal but there's satisfaction, enjoyment and worth-while-ness in the effort. It was much like a family reunion and indeed good interaction and input for the children.

At that time, I baked the ham; (Taking the skin off, scoring the fat and placing cloves into the ham; glazing with pineapple juice, syrup or sugar. Now we buy the baked ham. Nevertheless, I still bake the turkey and make the stuffing and giblet gravy. At this point, I do not have the desire or energy to do much in the department of Christmas decoration.

Christmas 1952, Kelly, Jr. was age four and Alfred Louis was one month, fifteen days; Pastor Coleman W. Kerry, Jr. and his brother, Rev. Norman Kerry came by our home to see what Santa Clause left under the tree for Kelly, Jr. and to find out his view of his infant brother, Alfred. They sat on the floor by the tree while conversing, looking at toys and playing games with Kelly Jr 'Such a nice thing to do', I thought.

In 1992, while my grandsons were still quite young, we always had a "Christmas Day Program" for the participation of everybody attending the Christmas dinner. At age four, Kelly, III recited the Lord's Prayer, Nathanael sung "Jingle Bells" and Desmond read the scripture (Isaiah 7:14 and later on St. Luke 2:4-14) Christmas carols such as: Joy to the World, Wish You a Merry Christmas, O Come, All Ye Faithful, Silent Night, The First Noel, God Rest You Merry Gentlemen, Deck the Halls and Hark! The Herald Angle Sing were sung by all in unison.

Rev. Zechariah Alexander, Jr., my brother-n-law, usually gave the Blessing. Unfortunately and sadly, my husband did not live to see his grandsons. After dinner, there was a look/see of gifts under the Christmas tree. Lots of conversation and recreation the entire day by everyone present.

It was indeed wonderful celebrating Christmas with family and friends. We exchanged good wishes, entertain visions of a better future for us and everyone else and we dedicate ourselves to do whatever is in our power for the realization of "peace on earth and good will toward men."

We have so much to be thankful for, therefore, we pause and count our blessings and good fortunes and reflect upon the many benefits and privileges which we enjoy. I am reminded of "If Every Day Were Christmas" by – Edgar DeWitt Jones:

> "If the spirit of Christmas were with us every day, some
> revolutionary events would occur:
> Selfishness would die a death of starvation.
> Avarice would be hung higher than Haman.
> Foolish pride would go down in crushing defeat.

Watch Night

HERE'S A LAUGHABLE incident which I recall regarding "Watch Night" service at Mount Moriah Primitive Baptist Church when I was about age 3 in 1927. I went to church with Grandma Lula and my Momma. I'd heard my elders talking about God and the New Year. The service had started, the spirit was high and a few minutes before midnight the congregation got down on their knees to pray. I kept watching the door because I expected to see in person God entering at the stroke of midnight. Of course I realize, that was indeed a very stupid thought which did not materialize. We just do not know what's going on in a child's mind.

Punishment

WHENEVER MY MOTHER indicated that she was getting a "switch for me" I immediately went to hide under my parent's bed. I'd watch Momma's feet and roll from side-to-side of the bed. This frustrated Momma because she could not reach me. When she finally caught me, it wasn't really that bad but I started hollering and crying as if she was destroying me before the switch even touched my body. It was only about three or four licks on the legs, hands or buttock. My father punished me only once. It was because I disobeyed his order to come into the house immediately. You see, I was at our back yard fence arguing with Margaret Burns across the fence and was a bit too slow doing what I was told to do by daddy.

Confession

I**N WRITING MY** memoir, I have decided to talk openly about something I have not spoken about in years. As a matter of fact, I try to forget and never talk about this chapter of my life. From around 1939 to 1943, my parents were associated with the whiskey business.

They sheltered me from their operation. I was confined to other rooms of our home and never was permitted around the customers consuming the product. Never did I serve, sell or handle any of the merchandise.

After entering college, I felt comfortable enough to talk to Daddy regarding the situation and told him how embarrassing it was for me; and ask him to stop selling whiskey. Daddy immediately complied with my request, which made me very happy. He had "a capacity to change, a capacity to learn and a capacity to listen, to be made more perfect".

Since then, I've read and heard about a number of famous families (i.e. the Kennedy family) and also there were numerous people in various communities throughout Charlotte-Mecklenburg County who were in the same position as we were, but have gone on to do great things in making the world a better place for everybody.

For example there were: The Mungo's on Baldwin Avenue, The Weatherspoon's on East Eight Street, Mrs. Mae Davis on North Caldwell Street, Ike and Ezell on East Tenth Street, Odessa and Buddy Young on North Alexander Street, Flum and Judge Williams on East Twelfth Street and John Henry and Lillie in Akins Alley

I suppose there comes a time when individuals do whatever it takes to survive. It's a matter of taking care of the family, putting food on the table, having a roof over your head, clothes, shoes and a coat to wear ... just reality.

Regret

THE PRIVILEGE OF spending much more valuable quality time with my very young grandsons, Nathanael & Kelly, III, is the one thing which I regret being deprived of due to circumstances far beyond my control. Attitudes, divorce and distance were major factors. I anticipated interacting and seeing my grandsons frequently and participating in many of their activities as they grew. That pleasure did not materialize; it's sad to say.

Regardless, I am truly thankful for the amount of enjoyable contacts we had, through the years, and have currently.

My grandsons know that I love them dearly. They are included in my daily prayers and I always remember their special events, birthdays and Christmas.

I am extremely proud of my grandson's achievements and wish them much success in all their future endeavors. God's blessings always!

Trip to South Africa

A T AGE 74, I accompanied Kelly, Jr. on a trip to Johannesburg, South Africa. This was my first trip out of the United States. Nevertheless, I looked forward to the experience and to seeing my grandson, Kelly, III, whom I had not seen in five years. Kelly, III and his mother, Veronica Motsepe left the U.S.A. a month or so before his fifth birthday and relocated in South Africa.

I recall boarding a plane in Charlotte, NC to Washington, D.C. where we boarded another plane to London, England. Now that was a huge airport. The largest I'd ever seen. After refreshing ourselves and relaxing in the hotel there for a few hours, we boarded a plane for Johannesburg, South Africa. As we came out of Custom's, the first voice we heard was Kelly, III shouting Daddy! Daddy! As he came under the rope to greet us. We were so glad to see each other; we hugged and generally made spectacles of ourselves. Veronica and three other family members were also at the airport to meet us. I am pleased to report that everything went well with everybody. The Motsepe family was hospitable and gracious to us. Veronica, Bridgette or Lilette were at the hotel each day to drive us to some place of interest or for some planed event. There was never a dull moment while we were there.

We saw Kelly, III every day. I really enjoyed our stay immensely. It was like visiting another city or state in America. The hotel, food, dress and homes were the same as ours. In Johannesburg I did not see anyone wearing the garments that we refer to as "African attire" in the U.S.A

Kelly, III, Veronica and sisters: Dr. Tshepo "Lilette" Ramaphosa[20] and Mrs. Bridgette Motsepe Radebe[21], parents: Mr. A.B.C. and Mrs. Garet "Kay" Motsepe (both now deceased) truly made us feel welcome. Each entertained us in their home and otherwise. We met some of their friends and other family members. We went to church, school, the zoo, shopping and lunch at the mall, out door theatre production and dinner. Flee market and tour of the country side and different areas.

I do not know what I would have done without assistance on this trip. I am so glade Kelly, Jr. was there to help with my carry on bag. I did not see any "Red Caps" to help like it was long ago. Therefore, one needs to pack lightly. There is long distant walking at the huge airports and crowded conditions.

We've seen Bridgette once since 1998; when she was in America on a short business trip and stopped in Charlotte, NC. She, Kelly. Jr., Margaret Woodard and I had lunch together.

Kelly, III visited us for a month in 2009. I surely was good to have him here in Charlotte with us again. We sincerely enjoyed his stay. Kelly. Jr. and Kelly, III are constantly in touch with each other. When it comes to technology, I am a bit slow. I don't even own a cell phone

Anyway, as long as memory lives, I'll always remember fondly that trip to South Africa. It was my once in a lifetime adventure and experience.

Pet Expressions

The following are expressions some of which I've used, others were heard during my lifetime or are from specified individuals:

Over the years, expressions of mine recalled:
"Rise, Shine and Give God the glory."

"I glory in your spunk."
(I'm happy, excited or rejoice for someone.)

When I arrive home from an automobile drive or destination, I'll say:
"Home Again! Home Again! Jiggerdy, Jig."

I suppose that implies I am happy and thankful to be back home safely.

As a warning, I sometime say:
"Remember, all closed eyes are not asleep."

While I'm on pet sayings, here's one from Plain Z:
"You can't take a Jack-ass and make a Race-horse out of him."

Now here's a funny occurrence which happen to me during the early days of my marriage:

Dr. John and Ruby Walker, friends from Washington, DC were visiting Kelly, Sr. and I during the early days of our marriage. I was asked to serve them beer. Now to show you just how inexperience I was, I filled two glasses with ice, poured beer over the ice and served it to our guest. That really was a "no – no." I didn't make that mistake again. We had a huge laugh at the incidence. In my defense, I don't drink beer, and never have. I didn't have the slightest idea about how it was supposed to be served.

Kelly, Jr. and I were talking about his freshman year at the University of North Carolina at Chapel Hill (UNC-CH). Out-of-the-blue, he said: "Why did you ask me if a person was black or white when I telephoned to inquire if I could bring someone home for a weekend visit? I noticed you always treated everybody the same."

Now that question, from my son, really disturbed me. Why did I ask? I do not know but I did … he's definitely correct. Perhaps it was due to the fact that integration was a new factor at that time. Before adulthood, I had little or no close contact with "white people". I grew up and lived in a segregated society. However, I was delighted with the change and therefore had to adjust. You may be sure, I was an active participant in the struggle up freedom's road for human and civil rights; otherwise, First Class Citizenship in every aspect of life. There was no turning back … just moving forward with justice for all people. I am a golden heritage life member, National Association for the Advancement of Colored People (NAACP); a former active Executive Board Member of the North Carolina State Conference of NAACP Branches and the Charlotte-Mecklenburg County NAACP Branch.

It might have been "curiosity or an inquiring mind that wanted to know". At any rate, I should have waited to see when they arrived instead of asking that particular question. Oh, but that is now hindsight. Nevertheless, every thing worked out just fine.

Kelly, Jr. graduated in 1966 from West Charlotte Senior High School but along the way attended both Second Ward and York Road High Schools; Received a Bachelor of Arts Degree in 1970 from the

University of North Carolina at Chapel Hill and a Master of Public Administration in 1973 from UNC-CH.

Kelly, Jr. attended Bethlehem Center Kindergarten, Myers Street Elementary School, Second Ward High School (7th & 8th grade), York Road Jr. High (9th grade) and West Charlotte Senior High School (10th to 12th grade).

Alfred Louis graduated in 1971 from West Charlotte Senior High School; received a Bachelor of Arts Degree – Political Science degree with a concentration in Criminal Justice from North Carolina Central University (NCCU) in Durham, North Carolina in 1975; Associate Degree in Mortuary Science, Gupton-Jones College of Mortuary Science, Atlanta, GA, 1978.

Alfred Louis attended Miss Blanche Tyson's Kindergarten, Myers Street Elementary School, University Park Elementary School, Northwest Junior High School and West Charlotte Senior High School.

A Tribute to
My Dear Husband,
"Mr. Civil Rights"

KELLY MILLER ALEXANDER, Sr. was born August 18, 1915 on an unpaved street lined with shot gun houses in the Brooklyn Section of Charlotte, to Zechariah Alexander, Sr. (1877-1954) and Louise Beatrice McCullough Alexander (1878-1955). He was the last of five children. As a very young child, Kelly became interested in public speaking. He would dress up in a robe and stand on the front porch of the family home or in front of a mirror and practice delivering a speech. His early education was in the public schools of the city. While attending Second Ward High School, he played half-back on the football team, where he earned the nickname "Shipwreck Kelly".

Kelly continued his academic and professional training at Tuskegee Institute in Alabama and at the Renouard College of Embalming, New York City.

His basic involvement in human and civil rights began in his youth because he disliked living in a segregated community. He fought vigorously against the patterns of racial discrimination and segregation that the black population accepted and had to live with legally.

In the 1930's, endowed with a 'marked adventurist inclination," young Kelly was hired by a Jewish merchant from New York and began traveling the country selling jewelry boxes. This is where he got an intimate look at discrimination. The two often were refused service at restaurants and rooms at hotels. It was those peculiar experiences that led him into the civil rights movement. During the 30's he wrote letters and articles to various newspapers and was invited to address various groups and churches.

In 1943, he dated me, Margaret Gilreece Alexander of Charlotte, North Carolina while I was attending North Carolina College for Negroes, (now North Carolina Central University, Durham, N.C.); and became engaged December 24, 1945. On April 21, 1946, Easter Sunday morning at 6:00 a.m. we were married. After the wedding, picture taking and breakfast served to the guest consisting of family members and a few friends, Kelly's father, (Plain Z sent him to work on a funeral and I (Margaret) went to church, Mt. Moriah Primitive Baptist Church where I was a member. We saw each other about 5:00 p.m. that day, after the funeral. What we considered our honeymoon was June, 1947, when we attended the 38th annual NAACP National Convention in Washington, D.C.

Kelly Alexander, Sr. has a long history of leadership with the NAACP. He revived and reorganized the Charlotte Branch in 1940. From this time on, he made the NAACP his major community organizational interest, with all his activities in the area of civil rights. He has served as Executive Secretary of the Charlotte Branch since its organization in 1940. He was elected president of the N.C. State Conference of NAACP Branches in 1948 and was re-elected each year until he retired in October, 1984.

He was first named to the National Board of Directors of NAACP in 1950 and became a life member in 1984. He was elected Vice Chairman in 1976, Elected Chairman, NAACP National Board of Directors in 1984 and re-elected in February, 1985. He served on many National Board Committees and contributed to the implementation of NAACP Policy and Procedures on the National, Regional, State and Local Levels. In all these years, Kelly M. Alexander, Sr. proved himself to be worthy and capable. He gave his best to a noble cause without a desire for any personal gain.

There was a time when the NAACP in Charlotte, North Carolina was the only open forum which paved the way for the meeting of minds – black and white. It was in this atmosphere that non-partisan political action through registration and voting was born and first encouraged. It was here that the stage was set for local desegregation of schools, hospitals, golf courses and other public facilities.

During the early days of his leadership, he was a lone voice in his community and state, speaking out against racial segregation, which was not only a dangerous endeavor but a most difficult task.

He and attorney Charles Bell were often mistaken for each other; both answered for the other. Both loved to smoke cigars and traveled in the same social and political circles. Both always maintained offices near each other, which was a continuing source of confusion to the general public.

Kelly, Sr. was ostracized by the power structure of his community and state, through intimidation and harassment. He fought courageously against racial segregation and discrimination in education, housing, employment and voter registration.

He was successful in directing a campaign to secure the admittance of black patients to the tax supported Charlotte, N.C. Memorial Hospital on a non-segregated basis.

Over the years, Kelly, through the NAACP, attempted to better the lot of minorities through, "litigation, legislation and education".

His concern and sensitivity to the problems that faced black people in his community and state, during a most crucial period of racial discrimination and segregation in the body politics of his state, stimulated and motivated him to become directly involved in social change for his people.

Kelly, Sr. escaped being killed on many occasions. November 22, 1965, 2:20 am, night riders bombed the homes of four Black Civil

Rights Leaders in Charlotte, North Carolina and shattered the pride of the racially progressive city. They were: Kelly M. Alexander, Sr., Senator Fred D. Alexander[22], Attorney Julius L. Chambers and Dr. Reginald A. Hawkins.

Mayor Stan R. Brookshire asked residents of Charlotte to contribute to a fund to repair damaged homes. *The Charlotte Observer* announced an "Antiterrorism Fund" to provide a reward for information on the bombers.

To this day, the case is unsolved.

When our home was bombed at 2:00 am in 1965, Dr. James F. Wertz, then Pastor, Saint Paul Baptist Church came to sit with me, Kelly, Jr. and Alfred Louis while Kelly Sr. was outside accessing the damage done to our home and talking with the police and reporters. Dr. Wertz and Kelly, Sr. worked together in the National Association for the Advancement of Colored People (NAACP) and was also a friend of the family. Our Pastor, Rev. Coleman W. Kerry, Jr. was unable to get in but was across the street watching. Rev. Kerry, Jr. said, "The police would not permit me to cross the perimeter line to enter the residence". By the Grace of almighty God our lives were spared. We did not let the bombing deter our participation and involvement in the Human & Civil Right's Struggle up Freedom's Road.

Mr. Alexander received many citations and tributes for his long years of devoted, courageous and unselfish service to the cause of freedom. Among the many honors which have been conferred on him for his meritorious service are the following:

- Recipient of Citations from former Governor James B. Hunt, Jr. of North Carolina in 1979 and 1981.
- Former Governor James B. Hunt, Jr. proclaimed the week of August 18, 1984 as KELLY MILLER ALEXANDER, SR. WEEK' in North Carolina and commended this observance to the citizens.
- Citation from House of Representatives, State of South Carolina, September 21, 1983.

- Proclamation from Mecklenburg County North Carolina Government, September, 1984.
- Honorary Doctor of Laws Degree from Belmont Abbey College, Belmont, North Carolina, May 13, 1984.

Community activities have included: Board of Charlotte Health & Hospital Council; Board of Motions, Inc., a non-profit Housing & Economic Development Corporation; Committee of 100 for a Greater Charlotte; Co-chairman, Charlotte Council for Equal Business Opportunity; Member of Board of Directors, Charlotte Uptown Development Corporation; Board of Directors, The National Action Council for Minorities in Engineering, Inc. (NACME); Friends of Barber Scotia College, Concord, North Carolina.

August 18, 1984, the North Carolina State Conference of NAACP Branches presented the first KELLY MILLER ALEXANDER, SR. HUMANITARIAN AWARD to Kelly Miller Alexander, Sr. for Outstanding, Loyal and Dedicated Service 1942 -1984. This award was given annually, until 1996.

Mr. Alexander, a 33rd Degree Prince Hall Mason was active in fraternal, civic and religious activities in his community.

Kelly, Sr. lived long enough to see the community power structure that had fought him in the 50's and 60's embrace him in the 70's and 80's as a "positive force in the community".

On December 26. 1953, the *Carolina Times*, wrote about Kelly Alexander, candidate for city council:

"The one glimmer of hope for honest, courageous and dynamic leadership in Charlotte is that of Kelly Alexander, local undertaker and President of the State NAACP. But instead of throwing their support to him, the large crop of pseudo leaders continue to knife him in the back by sabotaging his effort to lead the big, dull sleeping mass of Charlotte Negroes out of the depths of lethargy and stagnation in which they now move and have their being.

Alexander has been able to get a few things done for his race in Charlotte, not because of the general help furnished him by other leading Negroes of the city but in spite of them. Charlotte needs some funerals among some Negroes who think they are big shots when they have actually been shot, shot to pieces with fear, selfishness and a lethargy that is keeping Negroes in the largest city and state in economic and political bondage."

To his dying day, Kelly remained as an active duty General in the Civil Rights Army. He departed this life on Tuesday, April 2, 1985 at his home.

To some Kelly, Sr. was a Doctor, Lawyer or Preacher;

To others he was a Counselor or loyal Friend;

To me he was a loving and devoted husband and a wonderful father to our sons.

I will conclude this tribute with one of my husband's favorite poems. The author is unknown.

Remember This

Be good but not too good – a little naughty, but not too naughty
Say a prayer if you feel that way, say damn
if it gives you consolation.

Be kind to the world always, if possible
– yet if you must be unkind,
Smash right and left, get it over and forget it.

LIVE YOUR LIFE so that at any hour you will be able to shake hands with yourself and try to accomplish at least one thing worth while each day. Then when your nights come you will be able to pull up the covers and say to yourself – "I have done my best".

Two Blessed Events

T HE TWO BLESSED events and bundles of joy were the birth of our two sons; Kelly Miller Alexander, Jr., 7lbs 12oz baby boy born October 17, 1948 and Alfred Louis Alexander, 6lbs 10oz baby boy born November 10, 1952. Both were born at Good Samaritan Hospital in Charlotte, N.C.

I recall occupying a private room for nine days with our first and seven days with our second son. Now days, you're up and out within a day or two. In the 1940's and 1950's, Good Samaritan was the only hospital open to Afro Americans.

They were literally born into a civil rights family. Kelly, Jr. and Alfred have been actively involved in Civil Rights since ages eleven and seven respectively.

Our son, Kelly, Jr. was President of the N,C. State Conference of NAACP Branches (1984 – 1996); a past Vice President, National NAACP Board of Directors; past Trustee, National Special Contribution Fund Committee and past Executive Director, Charlotte –Mecklenburg County Branch NAACP. Formally, he was also a youth member of the National NAACP Board of Directors and served on the National Youth Work Committee. A 32nd degree Prince Hall Mason; member of Charlotte Consistory #35; Z. Alexander Lodge #833 and Rosa M Morris OES Chapter #650.

At age eleven, Kelly, Jr. organized the Friendship Junior Youth Council of NAACP and was elected President. He was also President of the North Carolina State Youth Conference of NAACP.

Since 2008 Kelly, Jr. has been serving in the North Carolina House of Representatives as District 107 State Representative.

Our son, Alfred was President of the Charlotte-Mecklenburg County NAACP Branch (1990 – 1996); served as the branches Political Action Chairman and on its' Youth Work Committee for a number of years and was instrumental in bringing the 1st National NAACP Convention to Charlotte.

Alfred was a member of the National NAACP Security Team and also started and served as Director with NAACP Security on the State and Southeast Regional levels. He is a former National NAACP Youth Work Committee Chairman and member of the Special Contribution Fund (SCF) Board.

Member, Saint Paul Missionary Baptist Church and serves as a Deacon (ordained May 18, 2003) and on the Pauline Council (Executive Board) of the Church. A member of its' Business Ministry as well.

Alfred is also an avid supporter of Matthew 25:36 Ministries, Inc.

He is a 33rd Degree Prince Hall F&A. Mason; member, Charlotte Consistory No. 35; member, Ramesses Temple No. 51 and member, Rosa M. Morris Chapter No. 650, Order of Eastern Star; member of Z. Alexander, Sr. Lodge #833.

Member, Omega Pi Sigma Eta, Theta Chapter, National Morticians Fraternity. Member, Omega Psi Phi Fraternity, Pi Phi Chapter.

Life Member, North Carolina Central University Alumni Association, Inc.

Currently, Alfred is President of the family business.

Our sons benefited immensely, I believe, from the extended family relationship of their four grand parents, aunts, uncles and cousins. My cup overflows with joy and happiness, realizing that our sons have and are doing constructive things with their lives and filling their time with meaningful activities. May they continue on in this fashion with Gods' help.

Revelation

MANY PEOPLE DO not know that I had an older brother named Earl. When I was told of my brother, by my parents, I thought they were kidding me because I had never seen him anywhere. However, they explained that he died in infancy. A mid-wife cut his umbilical cord too short at birth. Mama and Daddy secured a doctor when I was born. Perhaps Earl and I will meet each other in heaven one day in the distant future. Anyway, I hope so.

Cooking: and an Overview
of Interesting Happenings

T HE VERY FIRST cake I made was more like sweetbread. I think
it was baked in the wrong type of container (a Pyrex dish).
At any rate, the cake sunk. I gave it to the kids playing in our back
yard. They enjoyed it.

After that failure, I learn to make very good cakes for many years;
until about three years ago during a rush preparing for our family
Christmas, my seven-flavor cake was a disaster. Nevertheless, I served
it for one of the deserts and called it "Holey Cake". It was eaten and
some asked for a second serving. Maybe they thought I was saying
"Holy Cake". I haven't made another cake since then. The baking
power was the culprit; I believe it was too long on the shelf and not
fresh enough to rise properly.

One Sunday morning, as newlywed, I was in the process of
preparing a hen for baking. I was experiencing difficulty in removing
the drum-sticks from under the narrow strip of skin on the chicken.
I knew they had to come out before washing and seasoning the
chicken. With no progress in getting them, I woke my husband to
come help with the situation. Thankfully, he was able to prevail. I
continued with the chore of washing, seasoning and baking the hen.
In the end, everything worked out well.

Now, on with the potato salad mixture; I boiled the white

potatoes and cut all the ingredients (mixed sweet pickles, pimentos, boiled eggs, onion & celery) then proceeded to mix them. Something was wrong; it would not stick together as it should; like the salad my mother made with the same ingredients. I put the bowl in the refrigerator. Later, when I took the bowl out of the refrigerator, it looked somewhat better. Then it dawned on me that I should have let the potatoes cool before adding the mayonnaise and relish dressing. Next time, I knew what to do; and the potato salad was very good.

When Kelly, Sr. brought home a duck for me to cook, I did not know how to cook it nor had I ever seen anyone else cook one. I had never eaten duck; therefore, I asked Momma Lou to cook the duck. Of course, I know now how to cook a duck and eat it also.

Liver was another disaster. As a newlywed, I bought pork liver instead of calf liver. It looked nice after cooking but eating it was something else. We chewed and chewed ... it was like rubber. I ended-up throwing it away. Momma had always cooked calf liver and I enjoyed it. From then on, my husband bought the meat for the family.

Kelly, Sr. really did most of the grocery shopping during our marriage. However I did the cooking. They tell me that I was on my way to becoming a master cook. At this point, I do very little cooking. I've done my share of cooking during my lifetime.

There was a time when I made pancakes from scratch. Our sons called them "Mothers' Pancakes". We seldom bought "Aunt Jemima's" pancake mix because mine was so good.

I remember standing by the stove with a double boiling pot stirring a mixture for lemon marine pie or banana pudding; even making yeast rolls and preparing a leg of lamb or ham back-in-the-day. Those good-ole-days are gone forever.

Kelly, Jr. and Alfred gave me a microwave for a gift when they were in high school. I was afraid to use it. Kelly, Sr. would not eat anything cooked in it, at that time. I was thinking seriously about having our sons return it and getting something else for my gift. On second thought, I decided to keep it because I realized that our sons really wanted one in the house to use. Over time, I began to use it more and more and eventually replaced it with another one. Now it seems like we can't do without a microwave. Funny, how we reconcile or adapt to things.

My Experiences as a Wife & Mother of Civil Rights Leaders

FIRST OF ALL, I must admit that I am one of those individuals who prefer working in the background and pushing others forward into the limelight. However, since my husband died (April 2, 1985); I found that some things just had to be done by me and I had to do my best to rise to the occasion.

My husband, had a long history of leadership with the National Association for the Advancement of Colored People; and at his death was Chairman of the NAACP National Board of Directors. He was a man of superlative high standards, complete integrity and a boundless enthusiasm for whatever task he took in hand. Indeed we are indebted to him for his courage, competency, compassion, vision and leadership.

My first NAACP State Convention was in 1946 shortly after our marriage in Rocky Mount, North Carolina. Dr. Marguerite Adams traveled with us there. This was a great educational experience for me; the guest speaker was Madison Jones, Director of NAACP Housing & Labor. Picture this: Newly married - green as grass - first time in an acquaintance home alone overnight - in an unfamiliar neighborhood; suddenly realizing that my husband was packing to go to Rocky Mount, for the state NAACP convention.

I thought it was going to be an overnight trip, but found out upon our arrival there that it was going to be a multi-day affair. Then too, it should have been obvious when Dr. Marguerite Adams, member, Executive Board of the Charlotte Mecklenburg County NAACP Branch, got in the car with luggage and a hat box. I should have gotten the message but it did not occur to me until we arrived in Rocky Mount.

Luckily for me that I had packed a change of clothes in my husband's bag. Coincidentally I had traveled in an aqua nylon jersey dress; so it stayed fresh looking the first day and evening. Also, packed was a yellow and black print crepe dress for the second day; which I wore with black paten leather pumps and handbag and a black straw hat with yellow trim. By the Grace and Mercy of Almighty God, I managed to survive the trip unscathed.

You see, I was ignorant of travel; I was not told, nor did I think to ask about distance, duration and type of events I would be participating in at the convention. You may be sure, I learned from that incident. Afterwards, I was always prepared in depth and in advance for conventions and conferences outside of the city.

My first National NAACP Convention was in 1947 in Washington, D.C. and Kelly, Sr. and I considered this as our honeymoon trip.

The National Convention was held at a church and we ate at a restaurant down the street and around the corner (approximately two blocks in walking distant). The delegates stayed in homes or in the one black hotel. Then SEGREGATION was the order of the day. This is when I first met Lucille Black, National Membership Director; Ruby Hurley, Southeast Regional Director and Gloster B. Current, who was then Youth Director.

During the 1940's and 1960's, while our sons were growing up, I served as Advisor to the Metropolitan and Friendship Junior Youth Councils of NAACP in Charlotte, N.C. We had several Church sponsored and community based Youth Councils in Charlotte-

Mecklenburg County. But in the latter 1970's I regret to say, we phased out those Councils and Chartered Junior and Senior High School NAACP Youth Councils and NAACP College Chapters.

By this time, both sons were off to college. As usual, I was busy at home being my husband's personal unpaid Secretary with everything that he was involved in (local, state and nationally); plus occasionally typing term-papers, book reports or thesis and etcetera for our sons who sent their college material home for me to type. Our sons also brought home laundry to be done while they were there for a week-end or holiday break. Frequently, classmates came along for the visit home.

When our sons were young, I stayed at home and kept the home fires burning while Kelly, Sr. and State Field Secretary Charles McLean traveled all over North Carolina in the interest of the NAACP.

Those were difficult days. There were many quick get-a-ways out of town after a dynamic speech; many harassing and threatening telephone calls. I was constantly on my knees praying for his safe return home to us. Our home was bombed on November 22, 1965 about 2 o'clock in the morning. Luckily and by the Grace of God, our lives were spared.

Whenever a State or Regional Convention met in Charlotte, N.C., my time was spent mostly in my kitchen cooking and serving meals to whomever Kelly, Sr. brought home; and frequently on the typewriter doing some last minute program to be distributed to the delegates.

I can visualize National Membership Director Ruby Hurley wearing a pair of Kelly, Sr.'s bedroom sippers helping me in the kitchen preparing breakfast for one shift after another at my dinning room table; and the National Youth Director Herbert Wright washing dishes in the sink. At that time, we did not have a dishwasher. In case you are wondering, my bedroom slippers were too small for Ruby.

I recall when times were a little tuff and the National Convention was approaching Kelly, Sr. would say "Well, I don't know if I'm going to the Convention this year or not". I think that was for my benefit because he knew that financially both of us could not attend. I would say, "Kelly, you know you are going to the Convention, if you have to walk". You may be assured, he attended every one. However before leaving Charlotte, he would see that everything was taken care of on the home - front. He telephoned every day to check with us. THE DIAMOND JUBLEE CELEBRATION was his last Annual National Convention in 1984. He died about tree months before the next National Convention (April 2, 1985).

This morning I thought about an incident which took place at an NAACP State Conference in North Carolina during a Luncheon. I was seated at a table a group of ladies of whom I did not know. At this point we had not introduced ourselves to each other. Across the table from me, I overheard two ladies conversation regarding my husband, who was then the North Carolina NAACP State President and was up front just crossing the floor. They said: "You know, we don't ever see his wife with him." Then I said: "You are looking at her now." Well! Those two looked as if they wanted to hide under the table. They were so embarrass and "were caught red-handed on the spot." Afterwards, I thought that I should not have said anything, just kept quite and listen to what else they had to say before introducing myself. Oh, but that's all water under the bridge. "The deed was done."

In 1959, I attended the NAACP's Golden Anniversary Annual National Convention in New York City. We stayed with my husbands' brother, Louis and his wife, Maude in Rutherford, New Jersey. Kelly, Sr. commuted to New York every day. I'd go to New York to attend the Pubic Mass Meetings, Luncheons, Fashion Show, Receptions and et cetera. Maud and Louis kept our sons busy with cook-outs, trips to the parks, movies and various places of interest.

At this time, Kelly, Sr. was the youngest member of the National NAACP Board of Directors. Later he was instrumental in getting the Board to add youth representation on the National NAACP Board of Directors.

At this Convention, I recall meeting Mrs. Roy Wilkins, Mrs. Clarence Mitchell, Jr. and her mother, Ma Jackson, Mrs. Ralph

Bunch, Mrs. Gloster B. Current, Mrs. Daisy Lampkin, Dr. H. Claude Hudson, Dr. Nathan Christopher & his family, Dr. Ulysses S. Wiggins, Mrs. Juanita Craft, Mrs. Lula White and Mrs. Maxine Smith to name a few.

I remember we closed with a large meeting at the Polo Grounds. We walked out to a platform situated on the field. A short time later, as the Guest Speaker was addressing the group, the rain came pouring down on us. Many of us vacated the platform and ran for cover; National NAACP Executive Secretary Roy Wilkins and a few brave souls, who had umbrellas, stayed on for the duration of the speech. There was covering over-head where the audience and delegates were seated; so they did not get wet.

In the 1960's, as Youth Council Advisor, I accompanied 45 Charlotte-Mecklenburg County Youth Council Members on a bus to the Annual National NAACP Convention in Washington, D.C. They were housed on the campus of Howard University. We sold candy and secured a bus for the round-trip with the proceeds. Any Council member selling three cases of candy (which totaled $90.00) was given a seat on the bus. We had the use of the bus every day during the Convention.

We visited the gravesite of Medgar Evers and President John F. Kennedy at Arlington Cemetery. They also met Robert Kennedy. Attending this convention was quite an educational experience for the group. They were impressed by the dignified, businesslike manner in which the youth officials conducted their National Annual Conference. The YOUTH PUBLIC MASS MEETING & YOUTH BANQUET are outstanding events to remember. I must say, through the years, I have thoroughly enjoyed attending many of the Youth Functions at the National Conventions. It is such a joy to see youth in action for the betterment of all mankind.

Each year we'd take a Bus load of Youth Council members to the "FREEDOM DAY CELEBRATION & MOTHER OF YEAR PROGRAM[23]" in Raleigh, N.C. to hear and meet some outstanding National Speaker. We usually had a group picture taken on the steps of the N. C. Municipal Auditorium where the program was held.

As a special project, THE FRIENDSHIP JUNIOR YOUTH COUNCIL – N.A.A.C.P. purchased a $500.00 NAACP Life Membership for its' sponsor, Friendship Missionary Baptist Church. The Junior Youth Council raised funds by sponsoring Car Washes, NAACP King & Queen Contest, Punch Hours, Teas and various dramatic productions and programs.

I remember typing affidavits for many applicants to desegregate the Charlotte-Mecklenburg County public schools after the 1954 Decision to integrate. Kelly, Sr. and I applied for our sons but were turned down because the School Board felt we lived closer to the predominantly black school.

In 1948, the Charlotte Branch NAACP employed Dr. Martin D. Jenkins to conduct a Survey & Report to examine the educational opportunities provided for whites & blacks in the public schools and to ascertain if facilities were equal during the 1947-1948 school year. As you might guess, there were marked inequalities in educational programs and facilities. I am pleased to say that I typed Dr. Jenkins' report.

Our door was always open for NAACP Committee meetings, activities and entertaining. Youth Council members made protest signs in our garage and mapped out strategies and position papers in our living room to present to the Board of Education, City Council or County Commission. Most of those papers were typed by yours truly.

We held NAACP Youth Leadership Training Workshops; directed various skits and programs; Held Door-to-door Register & Get-Out-the Vote Campaigns and signed up individuals for rides to the polls on Election Day.

I have enjoyed working with young people and seeing many of them mature, begin their own families and launch successful careers. It fills me with hope when I see young people doing something constructive with their life and filling time with meaningful activities.

Since my husbands' death, I've written the history of the Charlotte-Mecklenburg County Branch – NAACP and made several scrapbooks of the local Branch and the State Conference of Branches.

- I donated my late husbands' papers to the University of North Carolina at Charlotte (Atkins Library) for research and educational purposes.

- Margaret & Kelly Alexander Scholarship Awards in the amount of $1,000.00 each were given annually for several years to deserving students.

- I've participated in oral history for an ongoing project "Behind The Veil: Documenting African American Life in Jim Crow South" conducted by a team of researchers from Duke University, UNC-Chapel Hill, N. C. Central University and J, C. Smith University.

- I have been N. C. NAACP Historian; Chairperson of the Local Branch Life Membership Committee; Past Member of the local Branch Freedom Fund; WIN; Membership & Executive Board.

Our Block Neighbors

on Senior Drive

C. D. SPANGLES Construction Company had built houses in West Charlotte's University Park area. Kelly, Sr. purchased two lots on Senior Drive in order to build our home there in 1962.

We were so exited regarding our new brick ranch-style home with overhang roof, French doors and garage. At that time, it was not uncommon for people to show-up unannounced and ask for a tour of your new home. Occasionally, our young sons were asleep in their room or in the restroom when a door was suddenly flung open. They didn't say anything then; but over the years, I've heard quite a good deal about these unannounced disruptions.

The first neighbor to visit us in 1962 was Mrs. Richard Paysour. We knew her from Second Ward, our old neighborhood. She, her husband and family lived in the second house down the street from us. Mr. and Mrs. Eugene S. Potts were our next door neighbors. "Genial Gene", as he was called, was on radio station WGIV. Other neighbors were: The Gerald Elston Family; Mr. and Mrs. Ray L. Sinclair and Family; Mr. and Mrs. Elisha Hubbard and Family; The Alexander Starr Family; and Mr. and Mrs. Bruce Chandlers and Family. Our relatives, Fred D. & Mauvine Alexander and their daughter Theodora lived on the other side of us; they built and moved in the year before us. University Park Baptist Church (now the Park) maintained its parsonage at the corner of Senior Drive & Keller Avenue.

Only three of the original families are still living on the block. They are: the Hubbard's, Mr. Bruce Chandler, and Mrs. Willie Starr. Ms. Paysour is in a nursing home, presently.

Since the 1990's, the neighbors on each side of us are: Mrs. Norma J. Westmoreland and Mr. William and Mrs. Gladys Barksdale. We could not have better neighbors. They are really good people. Through the years, the Barksdale's have shared their garden fresh vegetables and fruits with us. Their daughter, Joann recently gave me a Valentine Day gift of cookies and a box of candy. Frequently, Norma purchase pastries, fruits or vegetables and share with me also. Norma and I are members of Friendship Missionary Baptist Church; as well as, Zack Alexander Assembly No. 35, Order of the Golden Circle and the Queen City Chapter of the National Women of Achievement. Inc. She's one of my riding friends.

Urban Renewal came through First Ward in the 1960's, and my parents sold their home at 709 East Eleventh Street and bought a house at 421 East 21st Street. At this time, my father transferred their pomegranate tree to our front yard. A sprig of the tree was planted on the South side of our house. Eventually, the main tree died but the sprig grew and bears fruit which we share with anybody who asks us for pomegranates.

Special Individuals

O F THE SPECIAL individuals in my life, I am going to name only two; my mother's sister, Aunt Odessa Wallace Cloud; and secondly, a companion of my father, after my mother died, Mrs. Mary E. 'Lizzie' Haggins. They were and are like second mothers to me. Neither had children of their own; therefore, I became their daughter. Aunt Odessa died December 29, 1989. I was with her until the end of her life and remember her warmly.

Some of Aunt Odessa's favorite sayings were: "We brought nothing into the world and will take nothing out – so do good and constructive things while we live." "Do good for evil. Do not hold malice in your heart but rather treat others as you wish to be treated." "Always say 'thank you' when someone gives you something". "It's better and more Blessed to give than to receive."

Lizzie and I are still very close, in touch and love each other dearly. She turned ninety-three years of age in 2012; which is indeed a blessing. Both of us are getting over-in-the-evening age wise; and do not see each other as often as we would like, but we do use the telephone frequently. Lizzie doesn't drive anymore; and I have never driven. Nevertheless, we are on the same wavelength of understanding each other's situation and circumstances.

I telephoned "Lizzie" to get her take on living in First Ward as a youth. The Stevenson Family resided at 830 North Alexander Street (corner, North Alexander and East Twelfth Streets). I walked past their home daily in my youth going to Alexander Street Elementary School.

Lizzie said, "I enjoyed being in First Ward. I had a good time there." Her mother, Mrs. Mary Stevenson, did washing and ironing for white folk; Lizzie helped a lot with the ironing. Neighbors knew each others family members and were very supportive and helpful in case of need. "If I had, you had" is how it was then. Nevertheless, her mother would not let her spend the night with anyone.

I was told that Lizzie and Isabelle came upon and raided their father's stash of B-flat bottles of whiskey, located in their toilet water tank, and drank a good portion of it. As a matter of fact, they got drunk and fell out. When their parents discovered them, they were scolded and given a whipping. Mr. Stevenson was upset about his "honey in the corn" being tampered with. I know that was a sight to behold.

Special Connections

TELEPHONE PAL – Michael Adams[24] is like a "Good Cheer Ambassador", "Inquiring Reporter" or "Investigator". I'm on his list of senior citizens who he calls frequently. He usually asks: "What did you have to eat today or yesterday?" "Where are you going today or have been recently?" What are you doing now or later? He gives you his take or view on everything. Then wonders why it's done this way?

We also discuss the weather. The conversation always end with "Have a nice day and God Bless!" He's the only person who greets me with my maiden and marriage name. He says: "Mrs. Margaret Alexander Alexander". Michael is indeed unique. He's an active member of The House of Prayer for All People.

Denise H. McIlwain and Carletta Judd are almost like daughters. They remember me yearly with beautiful greeting cards or a telephone call on – Mother's Day, Birthday, Valentine Day, Easter, and Thanksgiving/ Christmas; even a gift of chocolate candy once in a while. Now that's what I call kind and thoughtful.

Mary L. Peeler and Geneal F. Gregory – frequently remember my dear late husband, as well as his immediate family's contribution to the Civil Right's Struggle locally, state-wide, regionally and nationally. They, too, are veterans of the civil rights struggle.

Another protégée of my late husband, the Honorable Valerie C. Woodard, Charlotte-Mecklenburg County Commissioner is someone I wish to include. Valerie has gone on to glory; but she is not forgotten. I remember vividly one of her last acts of thoughtfulness and kindness toward me. She attended an annual national NAACP convention held in the southeast region; secured and brought me a calendar featuring a picture of my late husband who was at his death Chairman, National Board of Directors NAACP, on one of its' pages. You may be sure, I sincerely appreciated her thoughtfulness.

I wish to give a great big shout out with love and appreciation to everybody who calls me "Mother Margaret". I will not attempt to mention names for fear of neglecting someone; but I am sure you know who you are and I know you. I am so very pleased that you selected to bestow this honor on me. You did not have to do it, but you did. I sincerely thank you immensely!

I've known Margaret V. Woodard a long time. She's a lovely person (down-to-earth, thoughtful and very nice). She and my son, Kelly, Jr. were

friends before he married and became friends again after his devoice. I've found her to be respectable, reliable and sincere. She is almost like a daughter. Margaret treats me as if I'm her mother.

As a child, Margaret Woodard frequently visited her grandmother who lived in First Ward on East 6th St. She recalls the shot-gun houses and the vegetable and flower gardens in the area. When I shared with Margaret that I was writing a book, she reminded me of a few things to include, things which she remembered hearing me talk about. Now that shows her thoughtfulness. It also shows me that she is a good listener who retains information.

I feel a strong sisterly connection with Elizabeth Pendergrass, Robbie J. Banks and Evelyn G. Hollis. They are much younger women but we've worked together in the National Association for the Advancement of Colored People, the National Women of Achievement, Inc. and the Order of the Eastern Star for many years. Elizabeth Pendergrass is also God-daughter of my brother-in-law, Zechariah Alexander, Jr. As a matter of fact, Evelyn's mother lives in the neighborhood. Many years ago, Robbie invited me to dinner at her parents home while my husband and sons were out of town. You may be sure, I thoroughly enjoyed the delicious meal and the warm hospitality extended to me by the Johnson family. I have very pleasant memories of the afternoon spent with them.

Two other individuals of whom I feel a special connection are my great nephew, John Raeford Witherspoon, Jr. and his son, John, III. On September 5, 2012 John, III became age two. I have a framed picture of John, III in my bedroom. A birthday gift from me was a large tall clear plastic coco-cola bottle bank. I included some coins for John, III to put in his bank. I thought the gift would be a good incentive to practice saving early-on. Hope so anyway!

A relatively new young addition to our family circle is Aisha Dew. Our door stands open to Aisha. She feels relaxed comfortable and welcome at our home. The feeling is mutual. In the 1960's and 1970's, I was Advisor of the North Carolina NAACP Youth Council and Aisha's mother, Ruth Sloan, was a member of the group along with my sons.

This young lady graduated from Salem College in Winston Salem, North Carolina. In 2012, Aisha became the first Afro American women to be elected Chairman, Mecklenburg County Democratic Party. She did an extemporary job as Chair.

"Chief Operator", "Officer in Charge" or "Protector" are phases that describe Robert Ashton Walls. He's been with Alexander Funeral Home, Inc. for many years working closely with family members. He's somewhat like a brother or first cousin. When I was hospitalized in 2001 with a fractured femur, although he was confined to a wheelchair, his wife, Lillie Ann Walls, brought him to visit me. Every year, Robert delivers Christmas gifts to our family on Christmas Eve. Often he tells me, "There's an invisible fence surrounding your home for safety".

Luke Vasser was another individual who was almost like a "Big Brother" of mine. Long before I met Luke, he was a professional base-ball player, I was told. In retirement, he loved driving and drove cars frequently for Alexander Funeral Home, Inc. services. He also drove with my husband, to and from NAACP State and National Conventions and Regional Conferences. He called himself my chauffeur; "Driving Miss Daisy", he'd say. We'd laugh about that.

He also would drive my grandson back in forth between Atlanta and Charlotte. Luke died a few years ago. He is surely missed by all who loved and admired him; but God called him home to rest in peace.

Ms. Gertrude R. Hamilton, age 96, is another special lady and a friend. I admire her strength, stability and character. At this juncture, she uses a cane. (Walking Stick). Ms. Hamilton is a member of Saint Paul Baptist Church; which many years ago grew out of Mount Moriah Primitive Baptist Church. Dr. Gregory Moss is Pastor of St. Paul. Ms. Hamilton was also a personal friend of my brother-in-law, Rev. Zechariah Alexander, Jr. after his wife, Mildred Jeanette Alexander died in 1970. Ms. Gertrude R. Hamilton still travels frequently, has very good posture, looking good and is well-kept in her appearance. We see each other annually at Alfred and Helen Alexander's home for Thanksgiving dinner. Kelly, Jr. drives Ms. Hamilton and I to this event. We look forward to being there together enjoying the delicious meal and the good company and fellowship as well. Ms. G.R. Hamilton is indeed an inspiration to many who know her.

A recent friend is Lucinda Blue. She's truly a kind, thoughtful, considerate, helpful and generous person. Lucinda is much younger than me. Both of us are a member of Friendship Missionary Baptist Church and Alpha Lambda Omega Chapter, Alpha Kappa Alpha Sorority, Inc. She is married to Rev. William Blue and they have one son, Jarrod. Lucinda always says to me "If Kelly, Jr. or someone can get you there; I'll get you back home". That's reassuring and I appreciate same. We indeed like each other.

I do not drive; nor have I ever driven. We walked a lot when I was young. Our church and elementary school were in the neighborhood. The high school was only one mile and there were numerous short cuts on the way. Driver Education was not taught in school at that time. Then too, my father always had a car or truck, if I needed a ride. There were also streetcars or bus and taxies. Even when I was in College, after I married and had two sons most of the things I needed or places I wanted to go were in walking distance. My husband always had a car and there were cars at Alexander Funeral Home,

Inc., the family business. My sister-in-law, Mildred Alexander usually took me to sorority meetings in her car.

Currently, I depend on my sons and daughter-in-law to take me where I want or need to go. I feel truly blessed with family and extremely nice friends who accommodate me with a ride to meetings and events. "You didn't have to do it, but you did." I sincerely thank you for your kindness and thoughtfulness. I am so very grateful and appreciative.

I have mentioned some individual previously in this book but I have a few additions here and they are: Allegra M. Westbrooks, Eleanor A. Ervin, Barbara M. Stephens and Pauline Heading, my beautician.

++++++++++++++++++++

Various Events

A S A DEMOCRAT since the 1940's, a native Charlottean and supporter of President Barack Obama, I was pleased that the Democratic National Convention was held in Charlotte, North Carolina. At age 88, I felt the long distant walking and crowded condition would be too much for me. Therefore, I stayed at home and enjoyed watching the daily televised convention coverage.

On Sunday, September 2, 2012 the Friends of Fifty Committee welcome the Congressional Black Caucus and honored several distinguished leaders from North and South Carolina in the area of politics, law, religion, civil rights, medicine and sports. The Friends of Fifty Committee is made up of civic-minded professional individuals who have a long standing relationship with North Carolina. My late husband, Kelly Miller Alexander, Sr. was one of the honorees because of the outstanding accomplishment and valuable contributions that he made to this country. I accepted this recognition in Mr. Alexander's honor. Family members present were: Kelly M. Alexander, Jr., Alfred L. and Helen Alexander, Theodora A. Green, John R. and Tasha Weatherspoon, Jr. and Vera Mauvene Weatherspoon. The VIP Reception and gala featured a concert with Hill Harper hosting the ceremony at the Knight Theatre at Levine Center for the Arts, 430 South Tryon Street, Charlotte, North Carolina.

Last weekend was quite busy for this eighty-eight years young seasoned citizen; Saturday begun with Alpha Lambda Omega Chapter, Alpha Kappa Alpha Sorority meeting at 10:00 am. Approximately two hundred or more were in attendance at the University Place Charlotte Hilton Hotel. As usual, we had a very good meeting.

The 18th Annual P.E.A.R.L. Award Luncheon and Fashion Show started promptly at 11:30 am with a Reception. The Pursuit of Excellence in Achievement through Responsive Leadership Award (PEARL) was designed and developed by our chapter eighteen years ago with the intent of encouraging the values, ideals and precepts that encompass our purpose of being in "Service to all mankind." The Pearl Award recognize members of our community who exemplify outstanding leadership, excellence and achievement

2012 is also our 7th year of saluting emerging leaders and volunteers in order to encourage African American youth in the community. This is known as: "The Ivy Award".

The Luncheon Menu consisted of: A garden salad with House dressing, Entree: grilled chicken with mushroom gravy, Red Potatoes, Green Beans, Carrots, Bread, Desert: Key Lime Pie, Sweet Tea or Water.

The food was delicious; the fashion show was exciting, excellent and enjoyable. The event concluded at 2:00 pm.

On Sunday, October 14, 2012, 2:00pm, 400 East Martin Luther King, Jr. Blvd., Charlotte, North Carolina, Kelly, Jr. and I attended the dedication of the Friendship Missionary Baptist Church Historical Marker from the City of Charlotte. I've been a member of Friendship for sixty years. Kelly, Jr. literally grew up in Friendship and became a member in 1957 at age 9. Zechariah Alexander. Sr. enrolled him in the Cradle Roll Sunday School Department of Friendship Missionary Baptist Church immediately following his birth.

Friendship Baptist Church of Charlotte, North Carolina was organized in 1890. Forty (40) members withdrew by letter from First Baptist Church – Colored located at 1021 South Church Street, and organized a new church under the leadership of Rev. Allen L. Lewis. Sister Rosa Watson suggested the name Friendship, taken from the historic Friendship Baptist Church in Atlanta, Georgia.

For a while, these forty persons met in different homes and held services.

A lot was leased on South Caldwell Street from Rev T. R. Howell and a small structure began to take form. In a short while the building became inadequate and plans were made to accommodate the growing congregation. In 1893, a committee was successful in erecting the first permanent church sanctuary at 429 South Brevard Street, (corner of East First and South Brevard Streets). Rev. C. H. Williamson served as pastor of Friendship from 1893-1901.

As of August, 2006, our current location is 3400 Beatties Ford Road, Charlotte, North Carolina. Our 13th Pastor, Dr. Clifford Anthony Jones, Sr., who was called October, 1982, has led the way in establishment of many mission outreach programs including the Youth Opportunity University (Y.O.U.), the International Children's Outreach Ministry (I.C.O.M.), the Friendship Community Development Corporation (F.C.D.C.), the Genesis Charitable Fund for Catastrophe Relief, Inc. and My Sister's House, a transitional facility for homeless women and children.

The more than 8,000 members of the congregation are guided by these words of Pastor Jones, "Being led by the Spirit of Christ and understanding His will for us as a church, we are engaged in global ministry. Friendship Missionary Baptist Church is our name but we are called for a function that takes tantamount precedence over the legal status of our name. As a congregation, we are functionally the Body of Christ and members in particular. "For more than 122 years, Friendship has remained a church in the heart of the community with the community at its heart.

On Wednesday, October 10, 2012, Mrs. Sandra Eaves Belk, (Sister and Achiever) went home to be with the Lord and her funeral was Tuesday, October 16th, 1:00 PM at Saint Paul Baptist Church, Dr. Gregory K. Moss, Sr., Pastor officiating. She was a member of Rosa M. Morris Chapter, Number 650, Order of the Eastern Star, PHA, and a charter member of the Queen City Chapter, National Women of Achievement, Inc. (NWOA). Sandra will be missed by all of us. I knew her to be warm, kind, sincere and gentle lady of good report. Members of both groups participated in the Home going Celebration for Sister and Achiever Sandra E. Belk.

Three other special events worth mention which took place during the month were: Celebration of Kelly, Jr.'s 64th Birthday, October 17th. On October 18th, Kelly, Jr. and I stood in a long line at the Beatties Ford Road Library for two hours in order to cast our vote on the first day of early voting in Charlotte, N.C. We were proud to be there and to see such a large group of concerned citizens participating in our democracy. It's indeed wonderful to exercise our right to vote in America (the home of the free and the brave). Also, October 25th, is my grandson, Desmond Phifer's birthday.

Saturday, October 27, 2012 Kelly, Jr., Alfred Louis, Helen Alexander and I attended the 6th Annual Award and Benefit Banquet of Matthew 25:36 Ministries, Inc. "I was sick and you visited me".

Thus ministry, with a vision inspired by God, is dedicated to carrying the Gospel of Jesus Christ to all whose lives have been interrupted by illness that prevent them from continuing to live within the privacy of their home and have been laced in nursing home facilities. Mathew 25:36 Ministries, Inc. provide services that help our love ones adjust to their new home. The Ministry brings the church to them so that they can continue to worship our Lord and Savior Jesus Christ in prayer, songs and testimonies.

Matthew 25:36 Ministries, Inc. is presently ministering at seventeen facilities. Ministry visit include group worship, refreshments, individual and hospital visits. They provide memorial services; send flowers and cards to residents and families depending on occasions. They also provide spiritual support to residents and family members as well.

The mission of Matthew 25:36 Ministries, Inc. is: "To encourage, inspire, show love and be a friend. To console, bring joy, share God's word, sing and pray. To show empathy and compassion to individuals who suffer distressing, physical, mental or emotional problems and translate that compassion into cheerfully done deeds which reflect God's love and lift their spirits."

Minister Mary W. Caldwell is President and Founder and Pastor William Chandler is Vice President of Matthew 25:36 Ministries, Inc.

Alexander Funeral Home, Inc., Alfred L. Alexander, President is Banquet Title Sponsor and also a Table Sponsor of Matthew 25:36 Ministries, Inc.

I've attended every banquet thus far and have enjoyed each one. They get better and better each year! We are sincerely thankful and appreciative to Minister Caldwell and Pastor Chandler for their leadership in establishing Matthew 25:36 Ministries, Inc. and for their daily dedication and contribution in this worthwhile ministry. God's blessings always!

I received a letter dated October 17, 2012 from Stewart Gray, Preservation Planner of the Charlotte-Mecklenburg Historic Landmarks Commission

Regarding my home which had been identified by Charlotte-Mecklenburg Historic Landmarks Commission as being potentially eligible for local historic landmark designation. Presently, we are studying the facts concerning the Historic Landmarks status and haven't come to a definite conclusion as yet.

November 10th, 2012, my youngest son's 60th birthday! It was also a busy day for me beginning with a 1:00PM meeting of the Queen City Chapter, National Women Of Achievement, Inc. held at Saint Paul Baptist Church. The meeting was very productive.

At 4:30 PM, Kelly, Jr. and I attended a celebration of the History and Culture of the Historic West End sponsored by the Historic West End Neighborhood Association (HWENA) at East Stonewall AME Zion Church. The Master of Ceremony was Mr. Aaron McKeithan, Jr., Chairman, Historic West End Neighborhood Association (HWENA) meets monthly and shares information on areas of interest that effect the quality of life for individuals and families in the corridor. It also has an ongoing collaboration with Johnson C. Smith University (JCSU).

The Program included a presentation and viewing of the Documentary by Dr. Dan Morrill, Consulting Director, Charlotte-

Mecklenburg Historic Landmarks Commission. Included was a dinner buffet served with coffee and desert.

Also, at 6:30 PM, November 10, Kelly, Jr., Alfred Louis, Helen Alexander and I were present at the Blake Hotel, Charlotte, NC to celebrate, honor and commemorate the Leadership of Dr. Paul W. Drummond retirement (1999 to 2012) reception and dinner sponsored by First Mayfield Memorial Baptist Church. The Master of Ceremony was reverend Dennis R. Williams, Pastor, Faith Memorial Baptist Church, Charlotte, NC; Dr. C. Don Steger, Pastor, Reeder Memorial Baptist Church, Charlotte, NC as the Keynote Speaker. The "Black Tie" stellar event was enjoyable, well attended, thoughtful and deserving.

On November 17, 2012, Mrs. Norma J. Westmoreland and I attended the annual "Past Master Edward Newland Seniors and Widows Dinner" sponsored by the Worshipful Master, Wardens and Brothers of Unique Lodge No. 85 F. & A. Masons, Prince Hall Affiliation. As widow of Kelly M. Alexander, Sr. since 1985, I am a recipient of this wonderful caring team's kindness, thoughtfulness and generosity through the years. We are grateful, thankful and sincerely appreciative. God's blessings always!

Margaret's Journey

MARGARET GILREECE ALEXANDER-ALEXANDER was born
September 20, 1924, Charlotte, North Carolina; daughter of
Eulie Lester Gilreece (1902-1984) and Alberta Wallace Alexander
(1903-1976). Margaret attended Alexander Street Elementary School
and Second Ward High School graduating 12th grade in 1942. I was
crowned "May Queen in 1941 & 1942. This event was included in
a documentary film, "A Colored School". In 1993, I became a Life
Member of SWHS Alumni Foundation. Margaret received a B.S.
Degree in Commerce & Education from North Carolina College for
Negroes (now NCCU in Durham, NC) in 1946. In college, she was
inducted into Alpha Chi Chapter of Alpha Kappa Alpha Sorority,
Inc. (1945) and selected "Scroller Sweetheart" (1944). Now I am a
Golden Soror and Life Member of AKA Sorority. I am also a NCCU
Golden Eagle and Life Member. Margaret Alexander grew-up in
Mount Moriah Primitive Baptist Church; joined at age twelve. I
became an active member of Friendship Missionary Baptist Church,
Charlotte, NC in 1952. I am the widow of Kelly Miller Alexander, Sr.,
who at his death (April 2, 1985) was National Chairman, NAACP
Board of Directors. Two sons: Kelly M., Jr. and Alfred L. (Helen)
Alexander; Three grandsons: Nathanael, Kelly M.,III and Desmond.

From 1953 to 1996, Margaret G.A. Alexander voluntarily worked
diligently with the Charlotte Mecklenburg County Branch, National
Association for the Advancement of Colored People and the North
Carolina State Conference of NAACP Branches serving on their

Executive Boards and was N. C. NAACP Historian (1994-1996) and Chairman, 50th Anniversary Special Observance Committee in 1993. Youth Advisor, NAACP Youth Councils in Charlotte, NC from 1959-1971. Charlotte Mecklenburg County NAACP Membership Secretary for many years and a Golden Heritage NAACP Life Member. For 31 years, I was personal secretary for my husband, Kelly, Sr. and 4 years for son, Kelly, Jr.; both were NC State Conference NAACP Presidents. I am a consultant, Alexander Funeral Home, Inc., Charlotte, NC where son, Alfred is President. I was inducted into the Charlotte Mecklenburg County NAACP Branch Hall of Fame in 1990. My home was bombed November 22, 1965, 2:20 AM and by the grace of God no one was hurt. The case remains unresolved.

In 1957, Margaret Alexander became a Charter Member of Zack Alexander Assembly No. 35, O.G.C., P.H.A. serving as Associate Loyal Lady Ruler. In 2009, I was selected Honorary Past Loyal Lady Ruler. Through the years, she's chaired the Special Project Committee (Wrote & Directed "Tom Thumb Wedding" – 1958); Chaired Budget Committee (1986-1995; 2002-2011); Chaired, History Committee.

In 1975, Margaret G.A. Alexander became a Charter Member, Rosa M. Morris Chapter No. 650, Order of the Eastern Star, PHA serving as Associate Secretary. In 2002, I was selected Honorary Past Matron O.E.S. Also named in her honor is "The Margaret Alexanderettes Gleaner Branch No. 30, O.E.S." Throughout the years in Chapter No. 650, O.E.S., Margaret has served as: Past Public Relations Chairman; Past Member Service & Social Committees; Points: Ada, Ruth, Esther, Martha & Electra; Associate Worthy Matron, Warder, Conductress, Southeast Trustee and now Northwest Trustee; edited "Star Link" (Rosa Morris Newsletter – 2000-2001); Directed "Tom Thumb Wedding", September 24, 1977; Speaker, 16th Annual Fellowship chapter Dinner (1991); Editor of "The Liaison" (1998, 1989 & 1996), a publication of chapter news; Delivered Remarks, "Reflections of our Past", 18th annual Christmas Brunch; Wrote History of Chapter from 1975 to June 2002 and Chaired,

Scholarship Committee (2001-2003); Member Rosa M. Morris Book Club (2001).

Margaret G.A. Alexander is a Charter Member of both the Charlotte Chapter, National Women of Achievement, Inc. (1993) and the Queen City Chapter, NWOA, Inc. (2001); as well as, a Life Member, NWOA, Inc. Margaret was inducted into the "NWOA, Inc. Hall of Fame" in 2003 and Past Treasurer, Charlotte Chapter, NWOA Inc. (1993-2001).

Margaret Alexander is recipient of numerous awards and recognitions including:

- Alpha Lambda Omega Chapter, Alpha Kappa Alpha Sorority, Community Service 1988 and Exemplary Service Involvement 2001

- Became "A Diamond of Friendship Missionary Baptist Church" – August 16, 2010

- "2011 Hall of Fame Honoree as a pioneer and torch bearer"- Wadsworth Estate Foundation

- 2012 Who's Who In Black Charlotte – Living Legends – Civil Rights Activist – Mother of Civil Rights in North Carolina, (August 16, 2012)

- "Odyssey of a Women Award" Sigma Gamma Rho Sorority, Inc. Beta Omcron Sigma Chapter for Outstanding Service in Charlotte Community 2003

- "The Bakers' Dozen Plus" Community Service Award (2005), Cherry Community Organization, Inc.

- Certificate of Appreciation from Greater Mt. Moriah P. B. Church. Charlotte, NC, 1993

- "Essence of Freedom Award" North Carolina NAACP, (1994)

- "Order of the Long Leaf Pine – State of North Carolina", (1995)

- "Mother of Civil Rights Award – State of North Carolina", Silver Set Lodge No. 327, PHA, F & A Masons (1995)

- Personality of the Quarter, The Friendship Informer, Friendship Missionary Baptist Church, (1996)

- 40 years – Charter Member Plaque from Zack Alexander Assembly No. 35, OGC, (October 5, 1997)

- "Dr. Aaron E. Henry Lifetime Service Award", Southeast Region NAACP, (March 1 8, 2000)

- "Women In NAACP Service Award", Southeast Region NAACP (March 18, 2000)

My Interests, Activities & Volunteer Experiences include:

- Made History Scrapbooks of Charlotte-Mecklenburg County NAACP Branch and North Carolina State Conference of NAACP Branches and displayed same at the annual State Convention in Greenville, NC, October 1993.

- Donated "The Kelly M. Alexander, Sr. Papers" to the UNCC Atkins Library for research and educational purposes.

- Contributed family pictures to "The African American Album: The Black Experience in Charlotte & Mecklenburg County", 1992.

- Conferred with Artist Pat Ward Williams and contributed photographs and family history for "A Sentimental History: I Remember It Well", which was a 16 X 14 foot mixed media installation at the Carillon, The Hens & Walter Bechtler Gallery, Charlotte, NC Commissioned by Hest Properties, 1992.

- Contributed article to 1991 Centennial Directory of Mt. Moriah P. B. Church.

- Contributed to Centennial History of Friendship Missionary Baptist Church, 1990.

- History of Charlotte-Mecklenburg County Branch NAACP

- MGAA's Reflections on her days in Class 1942 at SWHS.

Today, September 20, 2013 is my 88th Birthday. I did not get to bed until after midnight last evening; therefore, Kelly, Jr. wished me "Happy Birthday before I retired. Alfred was the first person to phone this morning with "Happy Birthday". Soon after, my grandson, Nathanael telephoned from Marietta, Georgia to wish me a good day and happiness. Previously, I'd received cards, gifts and telephone calls from individuals and organizations of which I an affiliated including Friendship Missionary Baptist Church.

Alfred, Helen Kelly, Jr. and I dined at the Longhorn restaurant. Also, my grandson Desmond came by for a few moments to see us and wish me well on my special day. You may be sure; I enjoyed the delicious meal and the wonderful company. All-in-all, it was a glorious day for me to remember. I'm exceedingly thankful to God and Savior Jesus Christ for sparing me to be in the land of the living in order to celebrate my 88th Birthday. I am truly bless!

Tomorrow, four Service Committee members of Zack Alexander Assembly, No. 35, Order of the Golden Circle (Loyal Lady Priestess

Helen Alexander, Committee Chairman, Past Loyal Lady Ruler
Dorothy Cousar, Loyal Lady Treasurer Juanita Lowe and Honorary
Past Loyal Lady Ruler Margaret Alexander) are going to visit the
East Manor Nursing Home and deliver toiletries. socks and under
ware for the residents .

I am affectionately called "Mother Margaret" by numerous
individuals and "Mother of Civil Rights in North Carolina" by
others; I am known as the glue that keeps the Kelly Miller Alexander
Family together. She is committed to doing my bit to help make the
world a better place for all of us. She hopes you are too.

We must urge our course onward and upward; and "Continue to
let our light shine". With God's help and His blessings, we'll make it.

I will end this journey with expressions written on two plaques;
of which my husband bought many years ago and I keep one in the
foyer and the other in our bedroom.

A stanza from Our Family came from "Heartbeats" Hand Crafted
Plaques, Tulsa, Oklahoma. A stanza from I Believe ... plaque with
expressions of Mychal Wynn is from Pleasant Feelings Inc. of Beverly
Hills, California.

OUR FAMILY

God made us a family
We need one another
We love one another
We forgive one another

I Believe ...

If you are my friend,
Then you must always be honest with me
Even when it hurts

+++++++++++++++++++

It is my wish and prayer that we individually and collectively do everything possible for the betterment of all mankind. Our enthusiasm, determination and pursuit must never falter. We must have faith, persistence and patience to endure until victory is ours. LOVE, PEACE & UNITY!

Pictures

Mrs. Alberta Wallace Alexander
"Momma"

Mr. Eulte Lester Gillreece Alexander
Daddy"

Kelly Jr.: Kelly, Sr.: Margaret: Alfred

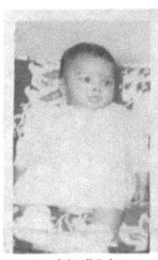

Infant Kelly, Jr.   Infant Alfred Louis

Graduation Picture
MARGARET GILMORE ALEXANDER
1938
Second Ward High School

Margaret G. Alexander during recess period on playground at Second Ward High School
in 1938. Margaret with son, Kelly Miller Alexander, Jr. (1 year 9 months) visiting her
parents at 709 East Eleventh Street, Charlotte, NC in 1950. A portion of Mt. Moriah P.B.
Church is also seen in the photograph.

113

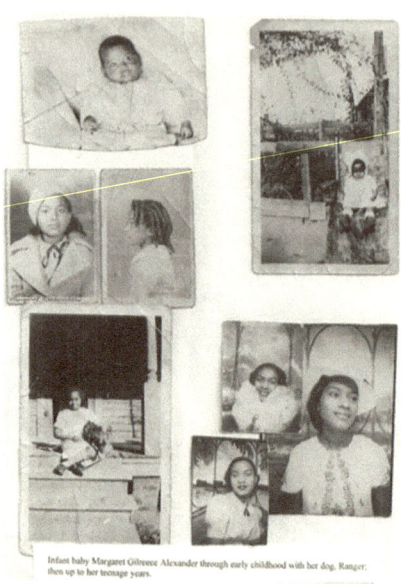

Infant baby Margaret Gilreese Alexander through early childhood with her dog, Ranger; then up to her teenage years.

Margaret G.A. Alexander and Kelly Miller Alexander on April 21, 1946, Easter Sunday morning after their marriage at 6:00 A.M.

All photographs of Margaret G.A. Alexander

1942 May Queen Court on front steps of Second Ward High School;
Margaret Gilreese Alexander is Queen

1985 - at the NAACP annual convention in Dallas, Texas where National Director
Benjamin H. Hooks introduced Mrs. Margaret G.A. Alexander, widow of the
late National Chairman, NAACP, Kelly Miller Alexander, Sr. after his
death. Mrs. Frances Hooks is seen in the background.

Kelly Miller Alexander, Sr. with son, Kelly M. Alexander, Jr. in 1948.

Kelly Miller Alexander, Jr., Margaret G.A. Alexander & Baby Alfred Louis Alexander visiting grandparents, Mrs. Alberta Wallace Alexander and Mr. Eulie Lester Gilreave Alexander at 709 East Eleven Street, Charlotte, N.C.

Kelly Miller Alexander, Sr. with sons: Alfred Louis and Kelly Miller, Jr. in our front yard playing in the snow at 415 East Stonewall Street, Charlotte, North Carolina.

Margaret G.A. Alexander in Baltimore, Md. standing in "The Kelly Miller Alexander, Sr., Circle" located in front of the NAACP national office building.

Margaret Gilreave Alexander Alexander

Kelly Miller Alexander, Sr.

116

Rep. Kelly M. Alexander,
State of North Carolina, District 107   Margaret G.A. Alexander   Alfred L. Alexander

Alfred & Helen Alexander   Margaret V. Woodard & Kelly M. Alexander, Jr

Aunt Odessia Wallace Cloud and her sister who is my mother, Alberta Wallace
Alexander; my father, Eulie Lester Gilbreece Alexander

Uncle James "Jimmy" Clarence Wallace

Uncle Walter "Sonny" Wallace

Aunt Virginia Holloway Wallace   Cousin Helen Jackson Laurel   Cousin Leonard Jackson

MARGARET G. A. ALEXANDER

Photo taken after tour of the City of Charlotte, NC and Lunch; (L to R) Maevette Dugan Alexander, Margaret G. A. Alexander, Mollie Moon of New York City, N.Y., Bobbie Alexander and Thelma Watkins.

Margaret G.A. Alexander, "Hall of Fame" inductee of Charlotte-Mecklenburg County, National Association for the Advancement of Colored People in 1990. Pictured L to R with her are: Geneal Frazier Gregory and Dora Ramsey Mason.

Margaret G.A Alexander "Hall of Fame" Inductee, National Women Of Achievement, Inc.,July 18, 2003, Houston, Texas; with daughter-in-law, Achiever Helen Anthony Alexander

Photographs of Margaret G.A. Alexander

118

Margaret Gilreece Alexander Alexander

Photographs of Margaret G.A. Alexander

Pictures of Margaret Gilreese Alexander Alexander

Inez Miller Dixon   Willie Mae Waddell Stroud

Nannie Little Snowden   Margaret G.A. Alexander

Margaret Gilreese Alexander Alexander

9th Grade Homeroom Class - Mrs. Laura Spears Malone, Teacher, 1939
Margaret Gilreese Alexander – First person on Left, Second Row

Margaret G. Alexander Alexander, 1942 graduate of North Carolina College for Negroes (now North Carolina Central University, Durham, North Carolina).

Son, Kelly Miller Alexander, Jr.

Son, Alfred Louis Alexander

Alfred Louis Alexander

Kelly Miller Alexander, Jr.

Alfred Louis Alexander, Margaret Gilmour Alexander Alexander & Kelly Miller Alexander, Jr.

My Parents - Eulie Lester Gilreeve Alexander (Daddy)
Alberta Wallace Alexander (Mumma)
Our oldest Son - Kelly M. Alexander, Jr.

"Pixie Z" Alexander & Louise B. McCullough Alexander;

Theodore Alexander and Kelly, Jr.

KMA, Jr., MDAA; KMA, Sr. & A.L.A.

Our Dog - Freckles (white with brown patches)

Margaret G. A. Alexander holding grandsons: Nathanael Maurice Alexander and Kelly Miller Alexander, III

Margaret G. A. Alexander celebrates birthday!

Margaret G.A. Alexander with sisters -in-law, Mildred McCullough Alexander and Maurene Dugas Alexander in 1946.

2014 picture of Margaret G. A. Alexander with sons: Kelly Miller, Jr. and Alfred Louis

Margaret G.A. Alexander and Rev. Emmet Burns, Guest Speaker at NAACP Freedom Fund Dinner sponsored by Charlotte-Mecklenburg County Branch in Charlotte, N. C.

Margaret G.A. Alexander at Charlotte-Mecklenburg County National Association for the Advancement of Colored People event.

(L to R) Margaret G.A. Alexander, second person from left, at NAACP National Convention with grandson , Nathanael Maurice Alexander, (L to R) Margaret Hickman Lyons, me, Helen Anthony Alexander and Ora Lomax, Security .

Margaret G. A. Alexander (second person on the left side of photo) at NAACP North Carolina State Conference of Branches Convention Freedom Fund Dinner with her grandson, Kelly Miller Alexander, III and his mother, Veronica Metoupe Alexander. Mary L. Peeler is seated at the right side of photo.

Margaret G.A. Alexander and Margaret Hickman-Evans, college roommates at their 1942 graduation.

Margaret G.A. Alexander, Hattie Plummer- Jones and

Margaret Hickman -Evans at their

College Class Reunion.

Margaret G.A. Alexander in Rutherford, New Jersey visiting brother and sister-in-law, Louis and Maude Alexander in 1947.

Alpha Chi Chapter
1945 & 1946 Alpha Kappa Alpha Sorority at North Carolina College for Negroes (now North Carolina Central University), Durham, NC

Margaret G.A. Alexander relaxing in chair at home

Margaret G.A. Alexander at NAACP National Annual Convention

Margaret G.A. Alexander

at Queen City, National Women Of Achievement meeting.

Margaret G.A. Alexander at home in Charlotte, NC ready for church.

Acknowledgement

I wish to thank my sons, Kelly Miller Alexander, Jr. and Alfred Louis Alexander for their help in proof-reading the manuscript. I could not have done it without your valuable support and cooperation.

Also, thanks to Helen T. Anthony Alexander, my lovely daughter-in-law, Alfred's devoted wife, who also read early drafts. Whenever Kelly, Jr. was not available to help with a computer problem, I called upon Helen to rescue me.

Thank you, Margaret V. Woodard for your consistent questions and periodic reminders of things to include.

Can you believe that, long before I completed writing the manuscript for my book, Helen and Margaret were already thinking, planning and asking me about the "book cover" and the possibility of a "book signing event". I found that endearing and laughable; like "Putting the cart before the horse". However, all were excited and kept "the faith".

My sincere appreciation to: Theoplis Ingram, John T. & Gladys A. Massey, Rosalie D. Meeks, Annie G. Hunter, Mary E.S. Haggins and Helen J. Laurel for talking with me about their experiences growing-up in First Ward.

Thanks to Elder Thomas W. Samuels for talking with me and suggesting members of Mt. Moriah P.B. Church whom I might call.

To everybody who participated in assisting me in anyway toward creating this book, know that I sincerely appreciate your cooperation, contribution and support.

THANK YOU, IMMENSELY!

Respectfully,
Margaret G.A. Alexander

Endnotes

<u>1</u> Hiram (Bro. Mack), Leonard, Tommie, Rufus, Helen, Kathryn (Didn't actually play with her because she was several years older)

<u>2</u> Willie Burton, Mabel, Ruth, Thelma, John Thomas (Sonny) Massey

<u>3</u> Louise McCullough Alexander, my husband's mother, attended this church

<u>4</u> Store Front Churches

<u>5</u> Pigeon coop on top of garage

<u>6</u> Dairy products were delivered by route salesmen to your door each week. Dairy sections in grocery stores were rare.

<u>7</u> In the early days, it helped that I was an only child.

<u>8</u> English poet and author, 1631-1700

<u>9</u> Today we would call this a multi-generational household

<u>10</u> Jewelry worn on the ears by women who did not have pierced ears, also called ear clips

<u>11</u> Modern zoning and licensing would prevent much of this activity from being carried out in residential neighborhoods today.

<u>12</u> The ritual of "foot washing" distinguished the members of primitive Baptist congregations from other Baptists. They were also very conservative in the role of women in the church, especially in the areas of dress.

<u>13</u> Alleys were short cuts people used to avoid going all the way around a block

<u>14</u> Incorporated on February 28, 1899, it was the first black owned insurance company in North Carolina

<u>15</u> Tom Simmons was an embalmer/funeral director, extremely active in the Masons

16 Printed in Baltimore, Maryland, the Afro was widely circulated within the black communities of the East Coast. Because "white" daily and afternoon papers ignored black social news, it was one of the few ways for blacks to communicate major community events.

17 President McKinley called for states to organize volunteer companies. Blacks in North Carolinas major cities answered the call. Governor Daniel L. Russell, who had been elected with the support of black votes created an all black volunteer regiment with black officers. Only three states created black regiments.

18 I didn't drive and never learned

19 Ate snacks on and off all day

20 Married to Cyril Ramaphosa

21 Married to South African political figure

22 His brother who broke racial barriers in the political field being elected to the Charlotte City Couyncil & the North Carolina Senate

23 Program started by Kelly Sr., to raise money for state and national NAACP programs. Program was so successful that it was copied by other NAACP state conferences.

24 Also known as "Funeral Boy"

www.ingramcontent.com/pod-product-compliance
Lightning Source LLC
Chambersburg PA
CBHW030304130626
46549CB00002B/686